Power

to Tread on

Serpents

Understanding and Using
Spiritual Authority

By David Sanzo

The High Places
By David Sanzo

Thanks to Billy Scott and Michael Johnson for their help on the cover of this book.

Unless otherwise identified, Scripture quotations are from the King James Version of the Bible. Scripture quotations identified NKJV are taken from the *New King James Version of the Bible:* © 1982 by Thomas Nelson, Inc., Nashville, TN
ISBN 0-9647343-8-9
For Worldwide Distribution
Printed in the U.S.A.

Spirit of Life Ministries
4830 Morwanda Dr.
Roanoke, VA 24017

Dedication

This book is lovingly dedicated to my parents, Anthony and Rosaria Sanzo. Thank you for raising me, loving me, and establishing within me very early in my life the fear of God and respect for all authority. God bless you richly in every area, Mom and Dad. I love you.

TABLE OF CONTENTS

FOREWORD

I would like to welcome the reader to this journey of exercising spiritual authority. When I initially began my study of spiritual authority, I did not consider that it would wind up in a book. I still have not concluded my study and, perhaps, I never will for I find that I am continually learning.

I began to study spiritual authority as a result of reading the first ten verses of Luke 7. In prayer and study, I received what I hold to be a revelation from God (better understood in theological circles as illumination). I was not taught this by man, as I had never heard it preached or taught to my knowledge. In fact, quite a number of ministers who have been in the ministry longer than I have been alive and have heard me speak on this subject have stated the same thing.

Now, by saying that this is a revelation, I am not claiming exclusive rights to this understanding. Indeed, after I had begun to preach it, I found the booklet, *The Authority of the Believer,* by Kenneth Hagin, and within a few months, Richard Gazowsky had written a book entitled, *Deep Calleth Deep.* Also, I understand that probably a good number of men of God had operated the principle of authority, whether they had the understanding or not. I recognize many others had also been given this insight and/or used it. But it was new to me.

This revelation started out as a single sermon, which gradually grew into several others. Then, as a student at Christian Life College in Stockton, California, I was required to write two theses, one of which I did on the subject of spiritual authority. This was to take care of one of my majors (Missions). This is the reason for the occasional reference to those involved in the work of missions or in the ministry (much of the references have been deleted but some still remain). Other insights were added to me over time until ultimately this book came into being.

Also, by calling this a revelation from God, I am not saying that there are not insights here which I have gleaned from other men of God. There are plenty of those. Many times I have been set in a certain direction by someone else's insights. And I owe much thanks to Dr. Dan Segraves, Executive Vice President of Christian Life College and, to me, the greatest teacher I know.

I want to encourage the reader to look up every reference of scripture that is not directly quoted in the following pages. This will help to instill the principle of authority much more deeply into your thinking. In addition, I encourage you to underline and to make notes. Finally, I recommend that you read the book through at least twice.

As a final note about the appendix - it is indeed beyond what I originally intended to communicate by this study. But since a discussion of spiritual authority would seem incomplete without a reference to what most Christians usually call to mind by the term "Spiritual Warfare" (including the idea of demonic princes in geographical areas), I included a few notes on the subject.

The first chapter will set the climate for the reason for this book. The next four will lay the foundation so that the last four will be most meaningful. And now, turn the page to begin. May the Lord bless you in all you do for Him.

David Sanzo

CHAPTER ONE

THE ROLE OF SIGNS AND WONDERS

In my walk with God, I learned early that I had to love God with all my heart, with all my soul, with all my mind, and with all my strength (Mark 12:28-30). As this began to take place in my life, I sincerely desired to please God with my actions, my words, my thoughts, my desires, and my motives - in essence, every part of my life. At first, I thought this included simply concepts of righteousness, that is, that which pertained to right and wrong. I eventually began to apply it to areas of wisdom and folly. I further grew to learn that "they that are in the flesh cannot please God" (Romans 8:8).

Then one day, the first part of Hebrews 11:6 stood out to me very strongly: "Without faith, it is impossible to please Him." For me to please God, I had to demonstrate faith - faith in God. I did not understand the full concept of pure and simple faith at the time, but I did associate it with signs, wonders, miracles, healings, etc. It seemed that was one of the only places I found a true emphasis on faith. So it began to quicken within me further a deep interest in the supernatural world and how to get it to work in my life.

Fortunately, I was involved in a church that believed in the miraculous and saw some miracles take place. There, I began to exercise my faith to see situations change in the lives of people. I came to be fascinated with the apostles, the early church, and, ultimately, the ministry of Jesus Christ. I saw where Jesus made the blind to see, the deaf to hear, the dumb to talk, the lame to walk, the lepers to be cleansed, the devils cast out, all manner of sick to be healed, and even the dead to be raised. The gospels are filled with these accounts. These great works of Jesus and the apostles caused the people to take notice and to follow Jesus or become Christians. Jesus had no problem finding a crowd to whom He could preach. The crowds were following Him.

Results of the Miracles of Jesus

In Matthew 4:23-25, Jesus healed all kinds of sicknesses and diseases, delivered people from various torments, healed lunatics, and cast out devils. The result was that "there followed him great multitudes of people from Galilee, and from Decapolis, and from Jerusalem, and from Judaea, and from beyond Jordan."

In Matthew 8, He healed a leper, one sick of the palsy, and Peter's wife's mother before healing all that were sick in the area (verse 16). In verse 18, great multitudes followed Him. He then calmed the sea and cast out the devils out of the two in the country of the Gergesenes. Of course, this did not hurt the size of the crowds.

In Matthew 9, He healed a lame man, causing the multitudes to marvel and glorify God. Later, He healed a woman with the issue of blood on the way to raising from the dead the daughter of a ruler. He continued doing great things, capturing the people's attention. In verse 35, He went through "all the cities, and villages" teaching, preaching, and "healing every sickness and every disease among the people." In verse 36, the result was that multitudes followed Him.

In the last two verses of Matthew 9, he desired that more laborers would help Him. So, in the beginning of chapter 10, he gave the twelve disciples "power against unclean spirits, to cast them out, and to heal all manner of sickness and all manner of disease."

In Matthew 11, John heard about the "**works** of Christ" and sent disciples to find out if Jesus was the Messiah. According to Luke 7:21 (Luke's account of the same story), Jesus performed numerous miracles in the same hour that John's disciples gave Jesus the message.

In Matthew 12:15, "great multitudes followed him, and he healed them all." As found in Matthew 13, He was able to teach the multitudes that followed Him.

In Matthew 14, He multiplied the bread and the fish and walked on water. Then, in the last two verses, the men of the whole country round about "brought unto him all that were diseased...and as many as touched [the hem of his garment] were made perfectly whole."

In Matthew 15, after a devil was cast out of a Canaanite woman's daughter, great multitudes followed Him "having with them those that were lame, blind, dumb, maimed, and many others..., and he healed them" (verse 30). This caused the multitude to glorify the God of Israel in the next verse. Before He sent the multitude away, He again multiplied the loaves and fish.

Here, in the book of Matthew, there is a shift in the recorded ministry of Jesus because His time drew near to be crucified. But it did not diminish the great miracles that took place nor the crowds that followed Him. Matthew 19:2 again refers to great multitudes following Him and being healed by Him. Matthew 20:29 refers to a great multitude following Him and tells of Him healing the two blind men outside Jericho. Even up to the point of His riding into Jerusalem on a colt, the people would "rejoice and praise God with a loud voice for all the mighty works that they had seen" (Luke 19:37). In fact, even in the last week of Jesus' life, after He had chased the moneychangers and company out of the temple, Matthew 21:14 states that "the blind and the lame came to him in the temple; and he healed them."

The other gospels are likewise filled with the same thought. Because of the many miracles that were performed and the spirit-anointed preaching, "the people pressed upon him to hear the word of God" (Luke 5:1). The people "were all amazed, and they glorified God" (Luke 5:26). In Luke 7:16, they glorified God because Jesus had raised a boy from the dead. Luke 9:43 records "they were all amazed at the mighty power of God." Luke 3:17 says, "all the people rejoiced for all the glorious things that were done by him." "Many believed in his name, when they saw the miracles which he did" (John 2:23).

A great crowd followed Jesus in John 6:2 "because they saw his miracles which he did on them that were diseased." Because of Lazarus, "many of the Jews went away, and believed on Jesus" (John 12:10-11). There is no doubt of the effect of Jesus' miracles on the common people of His day. They were powerfully drawn to Him in droves. And it caused them to believe in Him.

Some Did Not Believe

There were those in the gospels who did not believe, like some of the Pharisees and Sadducees. Their lack of belief was because they **refused** to believe, not because of simple doubt or skepticism. Although they saw many of the same signs and wonders, Jesus repeatedly rebuked them for they were always finding fault with the way He did things. They even accused Him of casting out devils by witchcraft (by the power of the devil).

> Jesus worked signs and wonders with a specific motive to help the people believe.

When the Bible speaks of unbelief, I believe it is not usually talking of a mere question of doubt or skepticism but of a refusal to believe. This is the reason Jesus "did not many mighty works there [in his home country] because of their unbelief" (Matthew 13:58). If they were going to refuse to believe, Jesus would not cast His pearls before swine.

When the Pharisees and Sadducees desired a sign from heaven from Jesus, He replied that their only sign would be the sign of the prophet Jonas (Matthew 16:1-4). This is a reference to the death, burial, and resurrection of Jesus Christ.[1] Because of their refusal to believe, Jesus would refuse to give them the sign for which they sought. Yet, he would point them to the greatest sign He was going to give to anyone, that of His resurrection from the dead.

---

[1] See Matthew 12:38-40

Jesus also repeatedly rebuked the disciples for their lack of faith (Matthew 17:14-20). He wanted them to demonstrate faith. He encouraged them to believe.

A point may be brought up concerning Christ's statement in John 4:48, "Except ye see signs and wonders, ye will not believe." He spoke this to a nobleman who came to Jesus asking Him to heal his son who was sick. But **this was not a rebuke.** In verse 50, Jesus

> There is no point in scripture where someone is rebuked for their exercise of faith.

told him to return home because his son would live. After making the previous statement, He turned right around and gave the nobleman the miracle he asked for. This is recorded as Jesus' second miracle after He came out of Judea into Galilee. He went on to do many others **because He wanted them to believe.**

In fact, in John 10:37-38 He said, "If I do not the works of my Father, believe me not. But if I do, though ye believe not me, **believe the works**: that ye may know, and believe, that the Father is in me, and I in him." Jesus told them *not* to believe if He did not do the great works. Jesus Himself placed a strong emphasis on the supernatural works. In John 14:11, He told Phillip, "Believe me that I am in the Father, and the Father in me: or else **believe me for the very work's sake.**" He pointed them to the works that He did. He was not afraid that they would turn into sign seekers. He wanted them to believe. And He purposefully pointed them to miracles as a tool to aid their faith.

Furthermore, the reason that some of the works of Jesus were written is that it might aid us in our faith. John 20:30-31 says, "And many other signs truly did Jesus in the presence of his disciples, which are not written in this book: But these are written, **that ye might believe** that Jesus is the Christ, the Son of God; and that believing ye might have life through his name." That was why Jesus did such great works. Not just to show off. He wanted to encourage faith.

Finally, there is no point in scripture where someone is rebuked for their exercise of faith. God is a rewarder of faith. Without faith, it is impossible to please Him. He would not contradict Himself.

Miracle of the Original Twelve

The book of Acts records that many miracles were performed, causing the conversion of many. Acts 2:43 says, "many wonders and signs were done by the apostles." Four verses later it says, "the Lord added to the church daily such as should be saved."

Acts 3:1-10 records where Peter demonstrated the power of God to heal a forty-year-old man who had been lame from his mother's womb. The result was that "many which heard the word believed; and the number of the men was about five thousand" (Acts 4:4). Counting women and children, there were multiplied thousands who believed just because of one single miracle.

> They can say "NO!" to our doctrine but they can never say "NO!" to our power!

When the Sanhedrin tried to call the apostles into question concerning their preaching that Jesus rose from the dead, they looked at the man that was healed and "they could say nothing against it" (Acts 4:14). In verse 16, they admitted that a "notable miracle" had been done by them and "we cannot deny it." They could say "no" to the apostles' doctrine but they could not say "no" to their power.

People may argue over whose doctrine is correct. They may dispute someone's theology and argue over whether Jesus or Allah is God or whether Jesus was just one of the "ascended masters" (New Age philosophy) but they cannot argue against evidence in front of their eyes. They can say "NO!" to our doctrine but they can never say "No!" to our power! How do you argue with a blind man who sees you? How do you argue with a deaf man who hears every word you say? How do you argue with a lame man who is dancing all around you? People cannot dispute a demonstration of power. Verse 21 and 22 says that "all men glorified God for that which was done. For the man was above forty years old, on whom this miracle of healing was shewed."

So what was the apostles' response? Stop the flow of miracles because the world might turn into a bunch of "sign seekers?" NO! They wanted to do more of this supernatural thing. They prayed that God would "grant unto thy servants, that with all boldness they may speak thy word, [how?] **By stretching forth thy** hand to heal; and that **signs and wonders may be done** by the name of thy holy child Jesus" (Acts 4: 29-30).

What was God's response? Was He disappointed with their request? Again, the answer is "NO!" He shook the place where they prayed, refilled them with the Holy Ghost, helped them to speak "the word of God with boldness... and **with great power** gave the apostles witness of the resurrection of the Lord Jesus" (Acts 4:31,33). God honored their request. He gave them a demonstration of His power.

Acts 5:12 says, "And by the hands of the apostles were many signs and wonders wrought among the people." The result was that " believers were the more added to the Lord, multitudes both of men and women" (Acts 5:14). According to the next two verses, they would bring all those who were sick and possessed with devils so that Peter's shadow would cover them "and they were healed every one." The apostles continued working miracles even beyond the initial stages of the church.

Miracles of Others

The working of miracles was not limited to the original twelve apostles. "Stephen, full of faith and power, did great wonders and miracles among the people" (Acts 6:8). Phillip did great miracles in Samaria. Signs, wonders, miracles, and the supernatural were the key to the revival and growth of the early church. This is contrary to the teaching that is

> Persecution has **never** caused revival. Signs and wonders and the moving of God's Spirit have always brought the revival.

predominant in modern (and anemic) Christianity which says that persecution brought their revival and will bring our revival. I disagree. Persecution has **never** brought revival. Signs and wonders and the moving of God's Spirit have always brought the revival. The Spirit of God brings revival, not persecution.

Often, the cynics will point to the persecution against the early church and say that it caused the revival. But let us take a closer look at the scriptures. Great revival was already taking place before the persecution began. The growth of the church had even spread beyond Jerusalem before the persecution. In Acts 5:14-15, the revival spread to all the cities around Jerusalem.

If we went back to the beginning of the church, we would find the growth affecting other places, even though it was primarily occurring in Jerusalem. The folks who were visiting Jerusalem on the day of Pentecost went back to their home towns - they had homes, family members who were not able to make the trip, friends, their businesses to attend to, etc. They would return and share the news of the events that had transpired at Jerusalem, i.e., they became witnesses. This undoubtedly produced revival and growth in their localities.

The Revival in Samaria

Let us look more closely at the revival in Samaria to see what caused it. Acts 8:6 says that "the people with one accord gave heed unto those things which Phillip spake, [why?] **hearing and seeing the miracles** which he did." The next verse says that many possessed with devils were delivered and "many taken with palsies, and that were lame, were healed."

Persecution did not cause the revival. The miracles sparked the faith of the Samaritans and caused the revival. If persecution causes revival, then I would go out into the streets and stir up as much persecution against the church as possible, because I want to see revival. But only a demonstration of the Spirit of God can bring revival.

Revivals Elsewhere

As a result of a lame man being healed in Acts 9:32-35, two whole cities "turned to the Lord." When Peter was used by God to raise Tabitha from the dead in the next seven verses, "it was known throughout all Joppa; and **many believed in the Lord.**"

In Acts 11:19-21, the believers went as far as Phenice, Cyprus, and Antioch. "And the hand of the Lord was with them: and a great number believed, and turned unto the Lord." The term "the hand of the Lord" (or "the hand of God") is used to refer to the power and authority of God. There was a great demonstration of God's power. In verse 24, Barnabas was described as being full of the Holy Ghost and of faith." The result was "much people was added unto the Lord."

This all happened because God was working with them, demonstrating the power of His Spirit - not because of the persecution. The only thing that persecution accomplished was to get the church scattered a little bit more. But the revival was already spreading beforehand as well as

> "The kingdom of God is not in word, but in power" (I Corinthians 4:20).

after the persecution subsided. They were starting with Jerusalem and expanding into Judea and Samaria before going to the uttermost parts of the earth (Acts 1:8). In addition, Paul and Barnabas did not embark on a missionary journey because of intense persecution but because of the leading of God's Spirit (Acts 13:1-4).

Paul saw tremendous revival not because of the persecution he faced but because of the working of the Spirit of God (Acts 14:3, 16:16-18, 19:11-12). Paul himself said that his speech and his preaching were "in demonstration of the Spirit and of power" (I Corinthians 2:4). He had said that he purposed not to come to them with words of man's wisdom. He was not trying to impress them with his great vocabulary or with his oratorical ability. He wanted them to notice the power of God being put on display.

According to the next verse, this was done so that the faith of those who heard him would not rest in the wisdom of men but in the power of God. If their faith would rest in the wisdom of men, then it would be forced to fail when the wisdom of men fails. On the other hand, if it rested in the power of God, it would be forced to fail when the power of God fails. But the difference is that the power of God will never fail. So their faith would never be forced to fail.

The Kingdom of God

Now, we believe in being a part of the kingdom of God. We believe that we must be born of the water and of the Spirit to enter into the kingdom of God (John 3:5). But sometimes we forget that "the kingdom of God is not in word, but in power" (I Corinthians 4:20). The preaching of the cross is the **power** of God to us who are saved (I Corinthians 1:18). This is not simply a code of morality. This is not about an intellectual agreement alone. This gospel is a powerful gospel. Daniel 11:32 states that "the people that do **know their God** shall **be strong and do exploits.**" If we are not strong and performing exploits, the problem is that we do not know God as we should.

Paul prayed for the Ephesian church that they would know "what is the exceeding greatness of his power to usward who believe, according to the working of his mighty power" (Ephesians 1:19). The word "power" in I Corinthians 1:18 and 4:20 and the word "working" in Ephesians 1:19 are all translated from the Greek root word *dunamis* which basically refers to a demonstration of energy, power that is put on display. This word will be discussed in more detail in Chapter 3. Basically, Paul wanted the church to know God's power to the point of demonstrating the supernatural abilities of God.

Effect of Miracles on a Modern Sinner

Even in our modern world, the effect of signs and wonders on people in helping them believe the Word of God is tremendous. I remember one incident that occurred while I was preaching on the West Coast about the healing power of God. When I finished preaching, I called for any that were sick or in pain to come to the front. One particular lady came to the front who, in reality, was probably in her late twenties (I found out later) but because of the abuse of drugs and a sinful lifestyle appeared to be in her fifties. She had been suffering from pain in her back for about three or four months. She did not truly believe that God would heal her. She came to the front only to be nice to me.

After praying for her, God reached down and immediately took all the pain away. Her mouth dropped open and she was amazed. She was in complete shock. She could not believe that God actually healed her just like the preacher had said He would. She pulled me aside several times while I was praying for others around the altar area to tell me just how amazed she really was.

While she was at the front, I led her in repentance and she committed her life to God. Finally, as the service settled down a little bit, she

> The story of the gospel of Jesus Christ is one that cannot be fully told in words; it must be demonstrated as well.

went back to her seat. The Holy Ghost then spoke to me that if I would lay hands on her, she would receive the gift of the Holy Ghost. I went back to her and asked her how she enjoyed the gift of healing that God had given to her. She proceeded once again to tell me just how thankful she really was.

I told her that God had another gift for her called the Holy Ghost, which she could receive if she lifted up her hands. She raised her hands toward heaven and I laid my hand on her. She began speaking in tongues within five seconds. The miracle had sparked her faith to be born again. I later found out that this was the first time she had come to church, hoping to find a last chance relief from drugs and a ruined life. It was her last hope. Thank God she found a reason to believe.

Effects of Miracles on a Modern Saint

Miracles even have a way of sparking faith in the people of God. I was in one church with a congregation numbering about 350 where I asked for the sick to come to the front to be healed (not just prayed for). At first only two or three came. But when the people heard that they had been healed completely, they began to come from all over the building.

One lady, who was facing surgery, decided she might as well give God a try. She had not been able to eat well for months because she could not swallow. Spicy foods were especially difficult. She was feeling tremendous pain in her throat and stomach. The doctors had examined her and were unable to find anything. They concluded that she had a rare disease that crippled the muscles in her esophagus.

We prayed and immediately God touched her. The pain left her completely. I told her it was a sign that the wonder had also been performed. As I found out later, she took my word for it. That afternoon she ate a full course meal full of violent spices - all with ease in swallowing and no pain in her stomach.

Then she decided to give it the ultimate test. For some reason, fruit seemed to have the worst effect on her. She ate a full bowl of fruit salad with no problem. God had healed her completely and saved her a huge medical bill that still would not have healed her. But seeing someone else healed sparked her faith to receive her miracle.

The Power of the Gospel

We must understand that the gospel of Jesus Christ is not just a story. The story of the gospel of Jesus Christ is one that cannot be fully told in words; it must be demonstrated as well. Paul told the Thessalonians "our gospel came not unto you in word only, but also **in power**, and in the Holy Ghost, and in much assurance" (I Thessalonians 1: 5). The power of God must accompany the telling of the gospel.

In Romans 15:18-19, Paul said that he made the Gentiles obedient (to the gospel) by word and deed. He described what he meant by saying "Through mighty signs and wonders, by the power of the Spirit of God: so that...I have **fully** preached the gospel of Christ." The gospel of Jesus Christ has not been fully and accurately told unless the power of the gospel accompanies it.

The Need for Signs and Wonders

We have a definite need in these last days for signs and wonders that will trigger a terrific revival and growth. We need a great demonstration of the supernatural power of God working in these days just as it did for the early church. We need a power that is in operation. We need more than a story of something that happened two thousand years ago and can be more easily doubted. We need a power that the world cannot deny. We need the notable miracles.

Spiritual authority is a vital part of the way miracles work and the way we can gain victory over the enemy so revival can take place. An understanding of the authority God has granted to the church helps enable us to perform our role better to see a greater revival. Hunger for a move of God that will change our world is the reason why this has been written.

> The gospel of Jesus Christ has not been fully and accurately told unless the power of the gospel accompanies it.

The church ought not to be simply a referral service. We refer the sick to the doctor, the troubled to the psychiatrist, those with marriage problems to marriage counselors, the financially troubled to financial counselors, etc. There may be nothing inherently wrong with any of this but the church ought to be more than a referral service. We ought to rise up in power and show that Jesus is the answer for the world today. We must fully and accurately preach the gospel of Jesus Christ.

CHAPTER TWO

INTRODUCTION TO
SPIRITUAL AUTHORITY

Luke 7:1-10 and Matthew 8:5-13 record the story of a centurion who had a sick servant and sent the elders of the Jews to entreat Jesus to come and heal the servant. The elders told Jesus that this man deserved such a miracle because of his love for the Jews. He had even financed one of their church buildings. It is funny how we often approach God for someone's healing by pointing out that they are worthy because they are such a good person, have lived for God a long time, or that their wonderful kindness has helped so many people. Fortunately, God is merciful with our sense of self-righteousness. In this case, Jesus obliged and went with them.

As they began to near the home of the centurion, they met some of the centurion's friends with a slightly different message. That message stated that Jesus was not to worry about coming to the home to heal the servant. The centurion corrected the statement of the elders saying that the truth was that he did not deserve the miracle. He did not even feel like he deserved the opportunity to meet this great prophet. The request now was just to speak the word only and the servant would be healed automatically.

The centurion explained the reason that he had believed this was possible was because he understood the principle of authority. He understood that when he spoke to a soldier to come or to go or to perform a task, the soldier obeyed and came or went or performed the task. The soldier obeyed because he was under the centurion's authority. The soldier

> Fortunately, God is very merciful with our sense of self-righteousness.

understood that the centurion was given authority from a higher power (Rome) and that, if he did not obey, that higher power (the Caesar in Rome) would come down with punishment.

The centurion used this illustration because he understood that Jesus had authority over all sicknesses and diseases. Jesus responded by saying that he had never seen so great faith in the entire nation of Israel. The centurion's understanding of the principle of authority helped him to have faith that Jesus' authority over the servant's sickness would work to heal the servant. Jesus tied his understanding of authority to his great faith.

I was moved to study this passage and the principle of authority in order to strengthen my faith. I believe that there needs to be a greater demonstration of the supernatural in the Church during these last days. This can only be accomplished through the exercise of faith. Paul wrote, "He therefore that ministereth to you the Spirit, and worketh miracles among you, doeth he it by the works of the law, or by the hearing of faith?" (Galatians 3:5). The obvious answer points to the relationship between faith and miracles.

Those involved in the work of the expansion of the gospel, whether at home or abroad, would benefit from a greater understanding of the principle of authority. Their new understanding would greatly enhance their faith, especially in regards to signs, wonders, miracles, and victory over demonic spirits (both in the lives of individuals and over geographical locations). The understanding of authority is important because God "does not deal with man by His power, but by His authority."[2]

Understanding authority is a key to knowing and understanding and following the will of God. This is of great importance to the missionary who is faced with certain decisions about how to react to the mandates of the government under which he is operating. This will also help the local pastor realize the values of obeying the local authorities and ordinances. It will also bring to greater light where we stand as far as the authority of the believer is concerned. Once that occurs, we can take advantage of properly using our spiritual authority to see God's kingdom advance.

> It is impossible for the carnal man to decipher the things of the spirit. It can only be done by the leading of the Holy Ghost.

Now, it is not possible to understand things of the Spirit by using our natural minds only, regardless of how brilliant we may be.

> "Eye hath not seen, nor ear heard, neither have entered into the heart of man, the things which God hath prepared for them that love him. But God hath revealed them unto us by his Spirit: for the Spirit searcheth all things, yea, the deep things of God. For what man knoweth the things of a man save the spirit of man which is in him? Even so the things of God knoweth no man, but the Spirit of God....But the natural man receiveth not the things of the Spirit of God: for they are foolishness unto him: neither can he know them, because they are spiritually discerned." (I Corinthians 2:9-11,14)

We must not lean to our own understanding when learning the things of the Spirit. It is impossible for the carnal man to decipher it. It can only be done by the leading of the Holy Ghost. We need to ask the Holy Ghost, given to guide us into all truth, to

---

[2] Larry Pollard, "Biblical Principles of Authority" (B.A.Thesis, Christian Life College, May, 1988), 18.

illuminate our minds and give us a revelation of our spiritual authority. Ask God right now to give you a "spirit of wisdom and revelation" to understand it (Ephesians 1: 15-17).

Then we need to take advantage of our authority and use it. As John Dawson has written, "We need to lift ourselves out of a self-centered spirituality - a mentality that says we are victims rather than warriors."[3] Remember, we are more than conquerors (Romans 8:37). It is not enough just to be sober, vigilant, alert, and aware of what the devil is doing. We must press into resisting him steadfast in the faith (I Peter 5: 8-9).

---

[3] John Dawson, *Taking Our Cities for God* (Lake Mary, FL: Creation House, 1989), 21.

CHAPTER THREE

THE MEANING OF AUTHORITY

I remember that it was usually my younger brother who got my older brother and I into trouble for eating various "goodies" when they were to be considered "off-limits" or were reserved for a special occasion. My older brother could wolf down the cookies we would sneak from the pantry within a couple of seconds. It was doubtful whether or not those cookies were ever chewed prior to digestion. It was even questionable whether or not he knew the art of chewing his food. He had the talent to make them disappear whole.

I usually managed to get my share chewed and swallowed just in time to escape discovery by my parents. But my younger brother was another story. Whereas my older brother could swallow things whole, my younger brother must have had what will someday be named Perpetual Chewing Syndrome. He could take what seemed like five minutes to chew and swallow a single cookie. Sooner or later one of my parents would walk in and we would get busted. It was not a great feeling knowing you had been caught doing something declared "off-limits." Eventually, we would learn to obey even when everything in us told us it was okay to disobey authority.

Have you ever considered what is it that gets you to obey the law even against your own wishes? Why do you listen when the government steps in and demands one-fourth of your paycheck (perhaps up to fifty percent) in the form of income taxes? What causes you to slow down speeding when you see a police car coming in the opposite direction? What causes you to listen to your supervisor at your job when he tells you to perform a task which is not to your liking or at an inconvenient time? What causes a child to listen to her parents' commands to go to bed at an early hour or to perform a chore when she would rather be playing with her friends? It is the concept of authority.

In our society we do not have as proper an understanding of authority as we should have. Rebellion runs rampant from the schoolrooms to the tax office, from the home to the streets, from our workplaces to the political demonstrations at Capitol Hill.

Rebellion is even idolized in some areas such as the world of hard rock and roll. The newspaper is not filled with articles of peace-loving citizens quietly submitting to the government. The six o'clock news is not concerned with reporting from a positive viewpoint in favor of the law-abiding citizens. Their stories are about glorifying the ones who are protesting a Supreme Court decision, demonstrating against a new bill in Congress, or revolting against police. Their stories encourage people to sympathize with those who want to overthrow "the establishment," with workers striking against employers, students rebelling against the teachers. They focus on revealing how there is corruption with those in authority, etc.

We don't hear about the students who are submitted to their teachers doing positive things but about the ones who are causing all the trouble. We have found ourselves in a society that is infatuated with rebellion. They teach us how to do what we want to do, to buck the system, to disregard our parents' desires, to back talk authority figures, to demand our rights instead of demonstrating obedience and submission to authority figures. Because of all this, our understanding of authority falls short.

Webster defines authority as power to require and receive submission; the right to expect obedience; superiority derived from status that carries with it the right to command and give final decisions; dominion, jurisdiction, delegated power over others, and right.[4] Someone in authority is one who has been endorsed by a higher power, empowered by him or her, and permitted to act on his or her behalf. They are able to act as if they had ability beyond what they really physically have. Authority implies the right to preside over and determine how something will be done.

The Strength of Authority

All authority is based on actual power to back itself up. This is why we will listen to the law even when it contradicts our own desires. It is why we allow the government to squeeze out twenty-five to fifty percent (or more) of our income often before we even see our paycheck. This is why we obey our boss at work and come in at a certain time every day even when it is not convenient. It is why little Johnny will go clean his room when he would rather be outside playing.

> All authority is based on actual power that can enforce it.

We understand the power behind the Internal Revenue Service, or the power of the police force that backs up the little ninety-eight pound female police officer. We recognize the power of employment and paycheck that our boss (or his supervisor) possesses. Even the child understands that his or her parents have physical power over him or her to make life more miserable for them if he or she does not obey, whether by spanking or revoking certain privileges. We listen to authority because we understand there is a greater power than ourselves that will work to back up the commands.

The Source of Authority

Part of the definition Webster applied to "authority" was "delegated power over others." Authority is usually delegated from something that has the ability to enforce the commands issued. Yet, not all people in positions of authority are there because they are the strongest men alive. It is not always a direct physical power that grants authority.

---

[4] "Authority," Webster's Third New International Dictionary.

Authority is usually delegated. Someone with greater authority gave them their authority. That someone, in turn, received his or her authority from a greater authority still. This ultimately traces back to the One who has all authority without it being given to Him because He has all the power

> All power finds its source in God. Therefore, all authority also finds its source in God.

and ability to back it up resident within Himself. He is completely self-sufficient. That someone is God. No one else has all authority that exists or all the ability to back it up.

God alone is omnipotent. There is no other god beside Him and there is none that we can liken unto Him (Isaiah 40:12-31, 42:9, 43:9-10, 13, 44:6, 24, 45:5-8, 18, 21-22, 46:9). The ultimate power of God is one of the strongest, one of the most foundational, and one of the most fundamental truths found in the Word of God. All power finds its source in God. Therefore, all authority also finds its source in God.

The concept of delegated authority starts in the beginning when God put Adam in the garden to dress it and keep it. Adam was given authority from the moment of his creation. God created him to have "dominion over the fish of the sea, and over the fowl of the air, and over every living thing that moveth upon the earth" (Genesis 1:27-28). God also had given man the command to subdue the earth earlier in the mentioned verses. Man was designed to exercise authority and power over the rest of God's creation.

However, man did not properly use the authority that God had given him; he did not obey God's commands. God gave Adam specific instructions of what he was able to do and what was not allowed (Genesis 2:15-17). Authority has always carried with it

> We must be good stewards of the authority granted to us.

duty or responsibility to achieve certain desired results and give account to the one who granted the authority (Hebrews 13:17). For whatever authority has been granted to us as individuals we must one day give account as to our results. We will be held accountable. We must be good stewards of the authority granted to us.

The Demands of Authority

The authority that we have been granted is representative of the authority above us or of the one who originally gave the authority. Romans 13:1-7 is an excellent study on authority in the natural realm for everyone involved in the missionary effort of the church and for every believer interested in increasing his own spiritual authority. It begins, "Let every soul be subject unto the higher powers. For there is no power but of God: the powers that be are ordained of God." The word "power" here refers to authority and not a physical ability. The English word "power" came from a French word used between the twelfth and sixteenth centuries. It has a strong meaning in the legal sense.

> The greatest demand of authority has always been obedience.

The Oxford English Dictionary defines authority as: "power or right to enforce obedience; position of power, delegated power; power to influence opinion, action or belief."[5] Again, notice the mention of delegated authority. Also, notice that it is the ability or right to enforce obedience. The greatest demand of authority has always been obedience. The authority of the government demands that we obey the laws dictated to us. The authority of our supervisors on the job requires that we obey. The authority of parents compels the children to obey. The authority of a military commander drives his subordinates to obey.

The Greek word behind "power" in Romans 13 is *exousia*. Strong's defines it as: "(in the sense of ability); privilege, i.e. (subj.) force, capacity, competency, freedom, or (obj.) mastery (...magistrate, superhuman, potentate, token of control), delegated influence: - authority, jurisdiction, liberty, power, right, strength."[6] *Exousia*, here, is referring to what we in the late twentieth century more clearly identify as authority. The stronger meaning behind the word refers to privilege, capacity, competency, freedom, mastery, delegated influence - all these point to an intangible, an abstract.

---

[5] "Power," Oxford English Dictionary.

[6] "Exousia," *The Exhaustive Concordance of the Bible* (Nashville: Abingdon Press, 1890).

Arndt/Gingrich defines it as follows: "the power a potter has over the clay, capability, control, ruling or official power, domain where power is exercised."[7] Ruling or official power places heavy emphasis on the idea of authority rather than the display of force. This is why mention is also made of the domain where power or the display of force is made.

When we deal with the authorities in the cities or countries where we are working, we are dealing with the delegated authority from God to that area to protect the interest of righteousness. We must recognize their authority. I will freely grant that there are many times when those in authority may be corrupted or use authority wrongfully. But we must still recognize their authority. This will be discussed more in detail in Chapter 4.

Kittel defines *exousia* in the following manner: "right to do something or the right to oversee something."[8] He states that it means authority, permission, and freedom to decide and to act. It refers to the possibility of action given authoritatively by the king, government, or the laws of state and conferring authority, freedom, and permission on corporations or individuals.

Moulton defines it as, "power, **ability, faculty,...** efficiency, energy,...**liberty, license,...authority, rule, dominion, jurisdiction,**"[9] [emphasis mine]. When used in plural form, it means authorities (as in referring to those in the position of office, usually in regard to the law), potentates (rulers), powers,...right, authority, full power,... privilege, prerogative.[10]

Clarifying the Concept of Authority

A distinction here needs to be made with another Greek word also often translated "power." This other word is *dunamis*. Whereas the emphasis of *exousia* is on the concept of authority, the emphasis of *dunamis* is on the forceful display of energy, the actual using of the physical ability. It is no longer the potential or the

---

[7] "Exousia," Arndt/Gingrich Greek Lexicon.

[8] "Exousia," Theological Dictionary of the New Testament.

[9] "Exousia," *The Analytical Greek Lexicon Revised* (Grand Rapids, MI: Zondervan Publishing House, 1978).

[10] *Ibid.*

representative of power referred to but rather the display or manifestation of that energy.

Exousia is the representative; *dunamis* is the real thing, the force behind *exousia*. It is not always easily separated from exousia but it is distinguishable. To go a step further, *exousia* is the representative of *dunamis*, especially when used in contrast with each other. *Dunamis* is the actual working that backs up *exousia*.

Moulton describes *dunamis* as power, strength, ability, efficacy (effect-producing), energy, meaning, purport of language, authority, might, power, majesty, a manifestation or instance of power, mighty means, omnipotence, authorities, miraculous power, a miracle, a worker of miracles.[11] *Dunamis* refers to power that is demonstrated by display. It is seen as external power. *Exousia* is demonstrated only by the fact that its commands are obeyed. It is seen as internal power. It refers to an area of control.

Sometimes *exousia* is used as a contrast to a self-asserted freedom, meaning that *exousia* is yours by right. This right is illustrated by the parents' right over their children, a master's right over his slave, an owner's right over his property, and an individual's right to personal liberty. When used in the plural, it refers to the rulers or the office of the state. It can imply a right given or protected by the law. In reference to God, it shows how His word is the authority of His power (Hebrews 1:3). In a general sense, it means power of disposal.

In the New Testament, *exousia* refers to that which decides. Man has been granted authority because he was created with a free will. He has authority over his will and has certain decisions to make which will greatly affect his future. Men and angels have only a sphere or realm or certain level of *exousia*. This is because God is the originator of all power and ability and man (as well as angels) has only a portion of it granted to him from God. God has complete authority while others have limited authority.

Exousia also has to do with the authority to act, legal jurisdiction, dominion, and the right to issue commands and give orders. Mark 2:10 refers to power to forgive sins. *Exousia* is used here. In that story, Jesus was demonstrating that He had the

---

[11] "Dunamis," *The Analytical Greek Lexicon Revised.*

authority and legal right to forgive sins because the offense was directed at Him. It came within His legal jurisdiction since He was God manifest in the flesh (I Timothy 3:16). He had both the authoritative ability and the working power to forgive sins. The writer uses the word *exousia* to encompass the meaning of both right and power.

So we see that *exousia* refers to the right to give the commands while *dunamis* refers to the demonstration of power that backs it up or enforces it. Now let us look at the effect of authority on our lives and on our walk with God. Let us start by exploring the effect our attitude towards authority has.

CHAPTER FOUR

ATTITUDES TOWARD AUTHORITY

In Romans 13:1, Paul is saying that every soul should be subject or submitted to the higher powers. Generally, this is referring to those in positions of authority. Specifically, it refers to those in legal position. The reason we are to be submitted to them is that "the powers that be" (an older English term used when referring to those in positions of authority) are ordained of God. They all find their root, their source, in God. "Since authority is of God, men can only assume authority as representative of God."[12] This is why we must give account to God for every use of our authority (Hebrews 13:17). Our authority represents God to those under our authority.

> "There is no authority except from God;
> all authorities have been instituted by Him.... God
> is above all authorities, and all authorities are
> under Him.... He upholds all things by the
> powerful word of His authority, even as He created

---

[12] Larry Pollard, 6.

them by the same word. His word of command is
authority."[13]

Here, Watchman Nee points out the principle that authority
is found in the word. Authority is evidenced by the word, by the
command given. It is found in a communication, usually written or
oral, although it can be otherwise as well. We know God's
authority is immense because His spoken word created the universe
and all that is in it.

Paul then stated in Romans 13:2 that whoever resisted
(rebelled against) the power (the authority) resisted (a refusal to
submit to, rebelled against) the ordinance of God (something God
had established and set in motion). The first obligation of all
believers in relation to authority is to submit to it, even in the case
of our missionaries living in
foreign countries where the
governments oppose God. The
greatest demand of authority is
submission - and we must
submit because it is the
ordinance of God, because

> Authority is always
> evidenced in a
> communication of some
> sort - usually a word,
> whether spoken or written.

authority is a representation of God (where it ultimately found its
source). Since authority is representative of God, our attitude
towards authority demonstrates our attitude towards God.

The Value of Submission

Nee distinguishes between submission and obedience.

"Submission is a matter of attitude, while
obedience is a matter of conduct. Peter and John
answered the Jewish religious council: 'Whether it
is right in the sight of God to hearken unto you
rather than unto God, judge ye' (Acts 4:19). Their
spirit was not rebellious, since they still submitted

---

[13] Watchman Nee, *Spiritual Authority* (New York: Christian Fellowship
Publishers, Inc. 1972), 22.

to those who were in authority. Obedience, however, cannot be absolute. Some authorities must be obeyed; while others should not be, especially in matters that touch on Christian fundamentals... Submission ought to be absolute. Sometimes obedience is submission, whereas at other times an inability to obey may still be submission. Even when making a suggestion, we should maintain an attitude of submission."[14]

It is not possible to submit to God's authority without also being submitted to God's delegated authority in man. A missionary is not submitted to God's authority when he rebels against the commands of the authorities in the area (excluding areas of Christian fundamentals). If he wants to be able to use authority that God has invested in the church, he must submit himself to all authorities above him.

> The greatest demand of authority is submission.

To verify this, Nee uses the example in Numbers 30 concerning a woman's vow. We understand that God viewed a vow as an unbreakable bond and even as sin (Numbers 30:2, Deuteronomy 23:21-23, Ecclesiastes 5:5). "While within her father's house in her youth a woman's vow or pledge was binding only if the father said nothing against it. If she were married, her vow had to be approved or disapproved by her husband.... Since the woman was under her husband's authority God would rather have her obey authority than maintain her vow."[15]

Verse two of Romans 13 then gives us the cost of rebellion against authority. Those that do resist or rebel will receive to themselves damnation. This does not necessarily refer to eternal damnation, although that will certainly be the case if rebellion is not repented of; but it is damnation nevertheless. Nee states, "There is no possibility of rebellion without judgment. The consequence of resisting authority is death. Man has no choice in the matter of

[14] *Ibid.*, 107-108..

[15] *Ibid.*, 73.

authority."[16] For those involved in missions, it is not a matter of choice whether we submit to the political authorities over us; it is a command. Being a part of the body of Christ is not a legitimate excuse for not being submitted to secular figures of authority.

There is no sacrifice that can make up for a lack of obedience. Authority requires obedience. No fasting, no prayer, no great offerings, no personal

> Since authority is representative of God, our attitude towards authority indicates our attitude towards God.

sacrifices, nothing pleases authority as much as obedience. Samuel told King Saul, "Hath the LORD as great delight in burnt offerings and sacrifices, as in obeying the voice of the LORD? Behold, to obey is better than sacrifice, and to hearken than the fat of rams" (I Samuel 15:22). The Lord is interested in our willingness to obey. Even if God speaks (as He did to Abraham) and tells us to sacrifice our only son on a nearby mountain, He is not as interested in the sacrifice as He is in our willingness to obey.

The wisest man who ever lived wrote a dissertation about the meaning of life, the purpose of living, and the value of mankind. After he had analyzed it, he decided to summarize his findings. He wrote, "Let us hear the conclusion of the whole matter: Fear God, and keep his commandments: for this is the whole duty of man" (Ecclesiastes 12:13). What God is requiring in man is not something beyond man's ability; it is simple obedience.

Faith is true when it obeys and is backed up by works (James 2:17, 26) and without it one cannot please God (Hebrews 11:6). God demands obedience to His Word. Furthermore, simply because authority is a representation of God, we must submit to it.

The Penalty of Rebellion

Damnation comes from the root word "damn." This means "to condemn to a punishment or fate...to bring condemnation or ruin upon."[17] In Roman law, the word *damnation* was used as a "condemnation, sentence, or judgment especially to pay

---

[16] *Ibid.,*62.
[17] "Damn," *Webster's Third New International Dictionary.*

damages."[18] Rebellion will always result in a penalty. That penalty will cause some degree of ruin in the person's life, and he or she will have to pay "damages."

> Even if God speaks (as He did to Abraham) and tells us to sacrifice our only son on a nearby mountain, He is not as interested in the sacrifice as He is in our willingness to obey.

The underlying Greek word behind "damnation" (which is *krima*) means "judgment; a sentence, award, administration of justice, execution of justice, a lawsuit, judicial visitation."[19] From the beginning there has been a penalty for not obeying the demands of authority (Genesis 2:16, 17). That penalty for Adam was death. The penalty is still death. "The wages of sin *is* death" (Romans 6:23). "Sin, when it is finished, bringeth forth death" (James 1:15). Disobedience is listed as one of the things those of a reprobate mind are given over to do by God. Paul said that they "are worthy of death" (Romans 1:28-32). The ultimate end of sin is death or destruction.

Respecting Spheres of Authority

We must always submit to the authority of others when we are in the realm where they exercise authority. Jesus, who possessed all power and authority in heaven and earth, submitted Himself to authority when in the domain of earthly man. His example is found in that He paid taxes "lest we offend them" (Matthew 17:27). When they asked Him a question regarding whether it was right to pay taxes to Caesar, Jesus responded by saying, "Render therefore unto Caesar the things which are Caesar's; and unto God the things that are God's (Matthew 22:21).

We may be granted certain authority through our positions. However, we must recognize the authority of others as well. There may be a case where one person is under your authority in one area but over you in another area, department, or situation. We must be humble enough to submit to them when in their sphere of authority.

---

[18] *Ibid.*

[19] "Krima," *The Analytical Greek Lexicon Revised.*

This may be illustrated by a pastor who may work on a secular job under one of the saints attending his church. While on the job, the pastor should recognize and submit to the authority of the saint. Likewise, the saint should submit to the pastor where work is not involved.

Exceptions on Obedience

The only exception where we have a right to violate the laws of the land is when it is in direct violation to the laws of God and conflicts with the God's authority. The apostles were faced with this predicament. The council asked them why they had disobeyed the order not to teach in the name of Jesus. They responded by saying, "We ought to obey God rather than men"

> When two laws come into conflict, the higher law takes control and rules over the lower law.

(Acts 5:29). This disobedience was allowed because the council's order contradicted the great commission that Jesus had given the disciples.

When two laws come into conflict, the higher law takes control and rules over the lower law. This is seen plainly by the court system of our land. If a state or federal law contradicts the Constitution (the highest law in our land) that law must be struck down. When involved in the work of missions, we can only righteously disobey a governmental command when their commands violate the higher authority, the Word of God, and then, it must still be with a humble and submitted spirit. It should be pointed out that just because we disobey one command that is not right does not give us the right to disobey other commands given to us that do not violate the Word of God.

Even when we must disobey one authority in order to line up with the Word of God (the higher authority) we should treat those offices and those who hold the office with respect. Paul exhibited this type of respect after he unknowingly ridiculed the high priest. When asked why he had spoken against the high priest, Paul did not defend his statement as being true. He apologized saying that he did not realize he was speaking to the high priest

> Satan fell because he desired to supersede the authority given to him and to set himself in the position of God.

(Acts 23:5). Then he quoted a commandment found in Exodus 22:28 saying, "Thou shalt not speak evil of the ruler of thy people." We are always to respect those in positions of authority simply because their authority represents God. This includes watching what we say in regards to them.

"God has established the structure and principle of human government. It is only a vehicle in which God can work. God's plan according to scripture is for man to have orderly government over His creation. This is done through the delegation of authority to man. This, of course, in no way implies that God approves of everything that man accomplishes or attempts in government. The government's authority is only blessed as long as it follows the biblical principles outlined in scripture."[20]

The Faces of Rebellion

Rebellion is not necessarily an action. It has more to do with an attitude, with a condition of the heart. Rebellion does entail action but action alone is not necessarily rebellion. An act that is performed contrary to certain laws is not rebellion if it was done in ignorance or because of deception. Rebellion has to do with the choice made by someone to directly counteract or frustrate those in authority.

Webster defines rebellion as "disobedience of a legal command."[21] Rebel is defined as follows: "to oppose or disobey one in authority or control; to show opposition; to feel or exhibit anger or revulsion."[22] Notice the focus on a feeling, on a state of mind. To

---

[20] Larry Pollard, 33.
[21] "Rebellion," *Webster's Third New International Dictionary.*
[22] "Rebel," *ibid.*

be rebellious is to be "resisting control; hostile to authority or traditions...; resisting treatment or management."[23]

Satan fell because he desired to supersede the authority given to him and to set himself in the position of God (Isaiah 14:12-15). He desired to usurp God's authority. The same spirit of rebellion is seen in man today when he disregards what God says about morality or right and wrong and sets up himself and his own reasoning abilities as the highest authority. Man is trying to throw off the need for submission to God as the only true authority. Man is refusing to be under God's "management."

Promoting Rebellion

Those involved in the work of God should be careful not to promote one with a rebellious spirit. It never pays to give someone authority so that they will be submitted to authority. This will only increase the magnitude of the problem. Money and power only magnify the attitudes one already possesses. They must always be submitted to authority before being given greater authority.

A rebellious spirit is often manifested by what someone says. "Out of the abundance of the heart the mouth speaketh" (Matthew 12:34). A rebellious tongue will curse men, "which are made after the

> We should be careful not to promote someone with a rebellious spirit.

similitude of God" (James 3:9, 10). This attitude has no place in the life of a believer, especially one involved in leadership, for it will only cause dissension and division in the body of Christ and hinder the cause of revival. Those who sow discord among the brethren are listed among the 7 things the Lord absolutely detests (Proverbs 6:16-19). "Today, many people find great joy in criticizing others [in authority] and disclosing their faults, as did Ham. This is a spirit of rebellion."[24]

---

[23] "Rebellious," *ibid.*

[24] Larry Pollard, 18.

Defects in Higher Authorities

Rebellion is often justified (in our eyes) because of the defects of the one in the position of authority. This is illustrated in the life of Ham (Genesis 9:20-27). Noah had a weakness with wine, drank too much and became drunk, and fell asleep being naked. This was obviously something that was not right. But Ham, instead

> We often feel like rebellion is justified because of flaws in those who are exercising authority. But there is no justifiable excuse for rebellion.

of trying to help with the situation, began to broadcast it by telling it to his two brothers. The two brothers manifested a tremendous respect for the authority figure found in their father when they went backward into the tent and laid a garment to cover Noah's nakedness. They were more interested in covering up a wrongdoing than in exposing it for all to see.

When Noah awoke and found out what had happened, he blessed the two boys who covered him and cursed Ham's son. This curse was that he was to be a servant (or slave) to his brothers (literally a slave to slaves). He was to be forever under their authority. This is not to teach us that we are to cover sin. Rather, it teaches us to respect authority and help minimize any problem or weakness that they may have.

Although there is some speculation that Ham engaged in other activities, an examination of the scripture shows that his only wrong explicitly recorded by the Bible was in telling his brothers. In doing this, he manifested a rebellious spirit. He vocally criticized an authority figure without doing something to remedy the situation. Christians should be aware of individuals who always criticize those in authority, for it is a sign of rebellion.

Nee notes that Ham failed to see the dignity of authority (the father is the authority in the home).[25] He further notes that "the flesh delights in seeing a defect in authority so as to throw off all restraint."[26] We feel that we are justified in our faults when we notice faults in authority figures. Just because authority may be in

---

[25] Watchman Nee, 28.
[26] *Ibid.*

the wrong is no excuse to get rid of all authority altogether. We should be checked in our spirit if we rejoice when we find defects in those who possess authority.

Those involved in missions should never get the idea that they are too far away to submit to authority, organizational or otherwise. You cannot operate properly in the body of Christ without submission. "Everyone who wishes to serve the Lord needs to meet authority. No one can serve in the spirit of lawlessness."[27]

> We may be anointed by God and be able to hear His voice but it does not justify a rebellious attitude.

Peter wrote that we were to subject ourselves to each other (I Peter 5:5). That is how much submission we should show. Even when holding a position of authority, a spirit of humility would keep us in subjection, for rebellion is a sign of pride. We may be anointed by God and be able to hear His voice but it does not justify a rebellious attitude.

"The example of Ham shows us that the one who is not subject to authority shall be slave to him who does obey authority."[28] Jesus taught this principle with regard to eternity (Luke 12:41-48, 19:12-24, Matthew 25:14-30). In these parables, those who were found doing the lord's will were given much authority. Those who were not found doing the lord's will were punished. Anything that they did possess was given to those who had done the lord's will.

Often, we justify our rebellion because of the defects of the one in authority. Gazowsky writes:

> "There is a lie that Satan communicates to most Christians who desire a promotion, or long for spiritual authority in the church.... The time that is most ripe for advancement is when those in leadership (or those in competition with you) sin. By exposing their sin to others you increase your image of self-righteousness, thereby showing

---

[27] *Ibid.*
[28] *Ibid.*

others your ability to lead and judge righteously. Nothing could be further from the truth."[29]

This was seen in the example of Ham and Noah (Genesis 9:20-27). One could argue that because Noah stumbled in righteous living, that Ham did no wrong since what he said was true. The weakness with this argument is that there is never a justifiable excuse for rebellion (which is distinguished from the times when we cannot submit to authority because it contradicts the Word of God). This is the case even when authority is in the wrong.

Those who enter a new area (whether city, state, or country) to do a work for the Lord must never allow themselves to be caught up with the spirit of rebellion against those placed in authority over them, whether in the organization or the civil governments. Rebellion may accomplish some things but it is abhorred by God and counted as a chief sin. The Bible counts it as sin on the same level as witchcraft (I Samuel 15:23). It was because of disobedience that Saul lost the kingship over the nation of Israel.

> We may be anointed by God and be able to hear His voice but it does not justify a rebellious attitude.

Gazowsky accurately asserts: "The main reason... that causes men to lose out with God and thereby forfeit spiritual authority, is rebellion. Remember: Any time you rebel, it is because you are **'right.' But rebellion is wrong**."[30] He further notes, "When rebellion comes on you, you feel so righteous that you honestly have a hard time discerning that the rebellion is an evil spirit. This is because rebellion is rooted in self-righteousness."[31]

We will feel that we are right in standing against authority but let us remember what happened to Miriam when she became upset with Moses for marrying an Ethiopian. She reacted with a spirit of rebellion. She was even correct in her official stance for the commandment was given that the Israelites were not to marry

---

[29] Richard Gazowsky, *Deep Calleth Deep* (Hong Kong: Voice of Pentecost, 1990), 24.

[30] *Ibid.,* 34.

[31] *Ibid.,* 50.

outside of their nation. She was saying, "Practice what you preach, Moses."

But her attitude resulted in God smiting her with leprosy because she opened her mouth against Moses. She felt justified because she was also a prophetess (Exodus 15:20, Numbers 12:2). However, she

> We may rebel because we are right. We may rebel because we are standing up for our rights. But rebellion is always wrong.

was wrong for acting with rebellion. We may be anointed by God and be able to hear His voice but it does not justify a rebellious attitude. God may have mightily used us in times past but it does not excuse the attitude of rebellion. Even if God has granted you spiritual authority, you must still guard against rebellion.

Overcome Evil with Good

The scripture gives some good examples of people who submitted themselves to authority even in the most difficult of situations. David was a man who was hunted by King Saul simply out of jealousy. Saul was trying to kill him. David, perhaps, could have been justified in our eyes if he would have killed Saul when given the opportunity. But when David's men suggested that it was the will of God that he kill Saul, David replied to them that this was not an option. He said, "The Lord forbid that I should do this thing unto my master [USING THIS TITLE, HE RECOGNIZES THE AUTHORITY OF SAUL], the LORD's anointed [NOW HE IS RECOGNIZING GOD'S ANOINTING ON SAUL'S LIFE], to stretch forth mine hand against him, seeing he is the anointed of the LORD" (I Samuel 24:6).

When presented with a second opportunity to kill him, David replied, "Who can stretch forth his hand against the LORD's anointed and be guiltless?" (I Samuel 26:9). You cannot walk in rebellion and still be innocent. We may rebel because we are right. We may rebel because we are standing up for our rights. But rebellion is always wrong.

Perhaps this is why Moses asked permission from Pharaoh to lead Israel out of Egypt. Though Pharaoh was a sinner, Moses was still under his legal authority. Even though Moses was doing the will of God in leading the children of Israel out of Egypt, he still needed Pharaoh's permission. "By Moses being obedient to Pharaoh's directive that he could not go, he submitted Pharaoh to the power of God."[32]

If you will walk being submissive to authority, you will force the authority above you who is in the wrong to answer to God for their wrongdoing. God will work all things out for the good. We must overcome evil with good. When authority is in the wrong, rebellion (evil) will not overcome it. Rebellion will not correct it. It can only be overcome with submission (good), even if it cannot be obedience. "Be not overcome of evil, but overcome evil with good" (Romans 12:21).

The Way Up Is Down

Watchman Nee points out, "It is absolutely essential that we be subject to authority before we exercise authority."[33] David submitted himself to authority in spite of adverse circumstances before he was ever able to sit on the throne of Israel. The effect of sowing and reaping is seen in his life. The people of Israel followed David with love and respect even when David failed.

Apostles Paul and Peter were also good examples of respect to authority even when those in authority were not deserving of it.

> "It is interesting to note that Paul in his letter to the Romans gives reference to obedience to civil government, but was himself living in persecution from the government. At that time the church was mainly made up of Jewish members, and the Jews were reluctant to have any dealings with Gentiles, let alone obey them. The Roman government's attitude towards the Jews and the church is revealed in passages like Acts 18:22, 'because that Claudius had commanded all Jews to

---

[32] *Ibid.*, 54.
[33] Watchman Nee, 44.

depart from Rome.' This command could very well be due to the fact that the church looked to Jesus and not Caesar as their King. 'And these all do contrary to the decrees of Caesar, saying that there is another king, one Jesus' (Acts 17:7)."[34]

Yet, in spite of this, Paul still recognized the value of submitting to and obeying authority. He wrote that every soul be subject to the higher powers. Peter, in the same situation, wrote that we were to submit ourselves to every ordinance of man for the Lord's sake (I Peter 2:13-20). In this passage, he went on to say that this was the will of God. We are to honor all men, and also the king. He then told servants to submit themselves to their masters. Paul

> We must overcome evil with good. When authority is in the wrong, rebellion (evil) will not overcome it. Rebellion will not correct it. It can only be overcome with submission (good), even if it cannot be obedience.

also tied submission to authority to being the will of God. He wrote that they were not to do it with eye-service, which is only doing it to look good in front of others, but to do it "as the servants of Christ, doing the will of God from the heart" (Ephesians 6:5-8) for God is always watching you.

Peter brings up an interesting point in his passage. He said there was no glory in suffering patiently for our faults. But if we suffered when we did not deserve it and took it patiently, "This is acceptable with God" (I Peter 2:19-20). Even when those in authority have faults and make mistakes and do wrong or injury against us, we are to take it patiently as David did.

This would help us not to develop roots of bitterness when it would be so easy to do so. "The attitude one shows to the authority above him is a direct reflection of his attitude toward God."[35] This should be kept in mind in all structures of authority: wife to husband, children to parents, citizens to civil authorities,

---

[34] *Ibid.*, 35.
[35] *Ibid.*, 41.

servants to masters, saints to the ministry, and all men to God's Word.

Peter referred to certain ones who were going to be reserved unto the day of judgment (I Peter 2:10-13). This included those who despised government (authority), were self-willed (not willing to submit to another's will - the concept of authority), and those who were not afraid to speak evil of dignities. The writer of Hebrews wrote saying that if we did not obey those who have the rule over us, it would be unprofitable for us (Hebrews 13:17). Other scriptures also tie obedience to authority with reward from the Lord (Ephesians 6:1-3, 5-8, Colossians 3:22-24).

Special consideration should be taken to realize that the word "servant" in these passages (Ephesians 6:5-8, Colossians 3:22-25) comes from the Greek word "doulos" meaning slave, not hired worker. Slaves were exhorted to obey their masters. It has been said that an examination of every culture where Christianity has projected a strong influence has done away with the practice of slavery. One of the reasons for this is that Christianity teaches the proper role of authority and the value of submitting to it.

Now, nowhere in the Bible does it condemn slavery as such. Instead of advocating rebelling and claiming one's rights, the Bible exhorts men to submit to the authorities above them. In the submission of slaves to authority, they became trustworthy and were allowed to take responsibility for certain actions and decisions to be made. This added responsibility carried with it authority. Thus, they were allowed to begin exercising some authority of their own.

This new authority or freedom to make certain decisions resulted from their proven trustworthiness. As they continued in their trustworthiness and faithfulness, they grew in their authority until ultimately they gained ultimate freedom. This is one example of how submission to authority can bring you more authority. Those involved in the ministry must realize this is the case in their field of labor. If they will submit to the authorities

> The way to increase your authority is to submit to authority.

above them, their own authority and liberty will be increased.

God's ways often work differently from our ways. The way up (to honor) is down (through humility). "Before honour is humility" (Proverbs 15:33b). " He that humbleth himself shall be exalted" (Luke 14:11b). "Humble yourselves in the sight of the Lord, and He shall lift you up" (James 4:10). " Humble yourselves therefore under the mighty hand of God, that He may exalt you in due time" (I Peter 5:6). Even Jesus first humbled Himself before exercising an authority over authority (Philippians 2:8-11, Matthew 28:18). He humbled Himself to become obedient to the death of the cross and was given a name or authority above every other name or authority. The way to increase your authority is to submit to authority.

CHAPTER FIVE

THE USE OF AUTHORITY

The proper understanding of authority not only entails submission to authority but also the proper exercise of authority. Authority can very easily be misused, especially on the missions field where one may be so far away from the organizational authority above him or her. It can also be easily misused in any other situation where the authority above us may be so far away (or is perceived to be detached from direct involvement) and unlikely to discipline us. A misunderstanding of authority causes its misuse and abuse, which, in turn, forms an incorrect relationship with the authorities above us. This, in turn, causes rejection by God, the loss of authority and its benefits, and even results in unanswered prayers (I Peter3:7).

This is seen in the life of King Saul who did not submit to the authority above him, which was represented by Samuel the prophet and the priests of the LORD in certain matters. God rejected him from being the permanent king over the Israelites. Saul, in turn, began to misuse his authority further for his own benefits and tried to kill some of his subjects (David, Jonathan, and Ahimelech with eighty-four other priests of the LORD) because of his jealousy and rage.

Those involved in leadership should remember never to exercise authority out of jealousy of another's talents or opportunities or because they are afraid of losing control. This is simply evidence that you do not know how to use authority or are refusing to use it properly.

Saul's jealousy of David's greater triumphs is evidence of his lack of understanding of the principle of authority. Our position of authority does not necessarily reflect our superiority over our subjects. We are simply stewards of God's authority in the matter.

Though Saul still remained king for a while, his authority kept weakening. When he needed an answer from God, he could not get

> When you exercise your authority out of jealousy of another's talents or opportunities or because you are afraid of losing control, it is proof you do not know how to use authority properly (or are unwilling to do so).

through. His prayers would not be answered. This almost drove him crazy.

Finally, he resorted to using the witch of Endor to find out what his plan of action should be. His wrong attitudes toward authority led to his misuse and abuse of authority. This, in turn, led to the ultimate weakening of his authority. The heart of the people continually shifted toward David. In the end, when Saul's prayers were hindered, he endorsed the ultimate form of rebellion - witchcraft.

Letting God Establish Our Authority

Our authority is not something that we should try to establish or assert right away as soon as it is granted to us. David refrained from killing Saul on two occasions when he had opportunity to do so. He was waiting on God to establish his authority. He refused to force the issue and assert his promised authority. Even when those in authority over you misuse and abuse their authority, you must not transgress by trying to take them down, especially if you are the next in line. You should submit yourself as much as possible until God puts you in place and establishes your authority. This will require both humility and patience. Nee observes:

> "David was one who was able to be subject to authority. He never annulled Saul's authority; he simply waited for God to secure his authority. He would not try to help God do it; he instead would willingly wait for God. Whoever is to be God's delegated authority must learn not to try to secure authority for himself."[36]

Political Versus Spiritual Authority

It is better for those involved in the work of God not to get involved with politicking for promotions or for greater authority among men. If it is offered to them they should carefully consider it and gratefully accept (unless believed to be contrary to the will of God). J. Oswald Sanders writes, "The true spiritual leader will never canvass for promotion."[37]

What the man of God is seeking is spiritual authority. Political authority is of little importance. To be a true spiritual leader of men is defined by Brengle (as quoted by Sanders) as " a leader whose power is recognized and felt in heaven, on earth and in hell."[38] He continues, "Religious position can be conferred by bishops and boards, but not spiritual authority, which is the prime essential of Christian leadership."[39] And spiritual authority is what we are interested in - authority that ultimately can be expressed over sicknesses, diseases, afflictions, infirmities, evil spirits, etc.

To gain authority (especially spiritual authority with God) you must submit to authority. Always submit to and respect authority and you will find that your own authority will be strengthened. When you disrespect authority, you undermine your own authority. For those in the military, if the colonel consistently

---

[36] *Ibid.,* 161.

[37] J. Oswald Sanders, *Spiritual Leadership* (Chicago: Moody Press, 1967 & 1980), 19.

[38] *Ibid.,* 26.

[39] *Ibid.,* 25-26.

gave orders that were contrary to the general's orders, it would not be too long before he would be called in by is superiors and questioned. He will probably be demoted and stripped of his rank (authority), possibly even court-martialed and be dishonorably discharged.

On the job, if a manager began to run the company contrary to the policies and wishes of the owner or board of directors, it would not be long before the owner would demote him or fire him altogether and find a new manager. He or she must exercise their new authority in submission to those who gave them their authority. In politics, things work the same way. No one is able to disobey the law without suffering the consequences, even if they are the ones that helped make the law.

Staying within Your Sphere of Authority

We must also learn to operate within the scope of our own authority. Nebuchadnezzar is one who tried to step out of the bounds of his own authority. He had a problem with pride. First, he built an image and commanded all to bow down and worship it (Daniel 3). This was outside the realm of his authority. Our authority is not to be used to elicit the love, adoration, and worship of those under it, though you will receive love, respect, and admiration if you use your authority correctly. But only God is to be

> A person in authority can only effectively and properly use that authority to the extent that he or she knows the will of God.

worshipped. Neither is the purpose of authority to gain great riches. Its purpose is not to benefit you personally. The purpose of authority is to serve others according to the will of God.

When Daniel prophesied of the coming judgment of God on Nebuchadnezzar in the next chapter, he warned him to repent and mend his ways (Daniel 4:27). Since he did not repent, in a moment of pride, his kingdom (sphere of authority) was taken from him. He even lost his sanity for seven years. God wanted him to know that there was a higher power and authority to which Nebuchadnezzar still had to be subject. We never become so big that we no longer need God. We never become so big that we do not need to submit to God's authority.

Limited Use of Authority

A person in authority can only effectively and properly use that authority to the extent that he knows the will of God. This is seen in the relationship of an ambassador or delegate with the nation that sent him. An ambassador is one who is sent from a king or nation to another nation to represent that first king or nation and their concerns. Barnes notes, "He is sent to do what the sovereign would himself do were he present."[40]

He is not to perform his own will but to perform the will of those who sent him. He is not to look for what pleases himself or benefits himself. He is not there to make new laws or make new terms without word (authority) from home to do so. If the ambassador does not know what is required of him he will not be able to effectively use his authority. But when he knows what is the will of those who sent him, he can work towards the accomplishments of that goal.

> We have a responsibility to use our authority in a way as to accomplish the will of God – to help, build up, make strong, and edify those under our authority.

"An ambassador has no independent position, no independent authority. What he is, he is because he represents the king or nation that has commissioned him to bear their message. Instructions are given him, and he must not exceed them.... He is the mouthpiece of others."[41]

To go beyond what he has been commissioned to do is to misuse his authority. As ambassadors of Christ (II Corinthians 5:20) the church has all the authority of our Lord, to represent Him

---

[40] Albert Barnes, *Barnes Notes* (Grand Rapids, MI: Baker Book House, 1884), 131.

[41] James Hastings, ed., *The Great Texts of the Bible,* vol. 16 (Grand Rapids, MI: William B Eerdmann's Publishing Company, n.d.), 211.

in this world. We can only use that authority effectively to the extent we know His will. Individually (for ourselves and for our church or organization), we must learn where the lines of authority are found and how it is to be used.

In the church, if we go beyond that which we have been commissioned to do by Jesus Christ, we have misused or abused our authority. A missionary who seeks to establish something other than the work of God in his area is stepping over the bounds of his authority. Even a secular leader can only properly use his or her authority to the extent they understand the will of God. Their authority must be used to advance the cause of righteousness. If they do not understand God's will or refuse to work His will, they are misusing or abusing their authority.

We must understand what kind of authority we possess, the extent of that authority, and where it ends. As long as you operate within this circle in obedience to God and submission to all delegated authority, you are safe and your authority will increase. On the other hand, if you overstep your authority, you will open yourself to failures, embarrassment, the loss of authority, and even personal hurt and ruin. We must recognize that a little authority that we may possess in one area does not open the whole world to our authority. We must know when to speak and when not to speak, when to act and when to be still.

The missionary (whether at home or abroad) must be careful not to overstep his authority. He or she must not fall into the trap of believing that because he or she is a "big shot" with some authority from God and, perhaps, his or her organization, that they have a right to disobey the local authorities. He or she must careful not to think that they can treat their congregation or the nationals as their servants.

This applies to all those in Christian leadership. A father and husband must not use his authority to treat his family as his slaves or "loyal subjects." He must not provoke his children to wrath. A pastor must not use his authority to manipulate his congregation for selfish purposes. In every case, there is a responsibility that accompanies our authority. We have a responsibility to use our authority in a way to do the will of God – to help, build up, make strong, and edify those under our authority.

We are not to take the world's concept of authority and bring it into the church. We are not to use authority for selfish purposes.

A Servant's Heart

"In the realm of politics and commerce, humility is a quality neither coveted or required. There the leader needs and seeks prominence and publicity. But in God's scale of values, humility stands very high."[42] In fact, I Peter 5:1-4 reminds us not to be lords or masters over those placed beneath our authority. We must have a servant's heart or mode of thinking, looking to serve, to help. We are to lead by example, not by force. Authority will carry its own force. We need not let our emotions run away with it. Sanders notes that "only once did Jesus say that He was leaving His disciples an example, and that was when He washed their feet (John 13:15) - an example of *servanthood*."[43]

Dawson uses the principle of a building to remind those of us in positions of authority to be humble. The roof is held up by the walls, which is on the foundation of the building. So authority is also held up by those underneath it who support it.[44] A pastor's authority over the local congregation and the foreign missionary's authority over the nationals are supported by those underneath the umbrella of their authority.

"Lord, help us to have a right attitude towards the authority figures you have placed in our lives. Help us to use the authority that we have been granted in a way that will honor you and cause people to love you, to draw near to you, and to commit to you. In Jesus' name."

---

[42] J. Oswald Sanders, 80.

[43] *Ibid.*, 32.

[44] John Dawson, 108.

CHAPTER SIX

CONNECTIONS TO THE SPIRITUAL WORLD

Everything in the natural world has a relation to the spiritual world as far as order is concerned. As authority works in the natural world, so it also works in the spiritual world. Paul said, "Wherefore ye must needs be subject, not only for wrath, but also for conscience sake" (Romans 13:5). We are to submit not only because we fear punishment for our wrongdoing but also for our conscience's sake.

We must understand that something beyond the physical world is being affected by our reaction to authority. Our authority over sicknesses and diseases, every evil spirit, and situations in our personal lives and the lives of others is affected by our attitude towards authority. Our authority is also affected by our use of the authority we possess. It is important we see this connection so that we may live properly and increase our authority spiritually. When we understand this relationship, we will know how to use it within the guidelines of the principle of authority. When we use our authority properly, we will be able to see God's kingdom work in a greater measure in our world.

Satan's Understanding

Satan seems to understand the principle of authority much better than many in the church do, even though he is the prince of rebellion and "the spirit that now worketh in the children of disobedience" (phesians 2:2). For example, when Satan wanted to afflict Job, he first had to get permission from the highest authority - the LORD. Afterwards, he was only able to go as far as the LORD had given him permission.

When God said that he was not allowed to touch Job's body, Satan did everything from destroying Job's wealth to killing his children, but he was not able to touch Job's health. Later, when he was given permission to touch his health but was forbidden to take his life, that was as much as Satan was able to do. This is the case even though Satan is a rebel at heart and the father of rebellion. He still knows that there are certain limits to which he can use his power. He recognizes that there is a greater power and authority than himself.

Another illustration is seen in Luke 4:30-37, which also shows the extent of Jesus' authority. The people who heard Jesus teach "were astonished at his doctrine: for his word was with power." The Greek word behind power is *exousia*, which places emphasis on authority, rule, dominion, and legal jurisdiction. Notice that mention is made only of His authority, not of the actual display of His power. This is because they had only heard His word. Again we are reminded that authority is found in a communication, usually a word, whether spoken or written.

> Satan seems to understand the principle of authority much better than many in the church do, even though he is the prince of rebellion.

Then a man possessed with a devil cried out. In the words recorded in verse 34, the devil recognized that Jesus had more power (ability or force), admitting that Jesus could destroy him. The devil asked if Jesus was going to destroy him. He recognized that Jesus had the power to do it.

The devil also recognized a greater authority in the person of Jesus Christ by attributing to Him the title "the Holy One of God." This title is a direct reference to the Supreme Being that rules the universe, the Yahweh of the Jewish Old Testament, here embodied in the flesh of Jesus Christ.

Jesus then cast the devil out of the man. The crowd's response was amazement at Jesus' word, "for with authority and power" He was able to perform this feat. In this phrase, the Greek word behind "power" is *dunamis*, which places its emphasis on the actual display of energy, the ability seen in action, the demonstration of the power. Jesus demonstrated His authority by His power. Again,

> Our authority as believers must be affirmed by a demonstration of the power of the Holy Ghost.

all authority must ultimately be backed up by power. So our authority as believers must be affirmed by a demonstration of the power of the Holy Ghost. It is not to be affirmed by our fleshly attempts to assert our authority. We are commissioned to operate in a spiritual kingdom. We have a spiritual authority. It must be backed up by spiritual power.

The Authority of Jesus' Name

The name of Jesus is the name that we have taken on through baptism in His name. That name has been given a standing above every other name or authority. Philippians 2:9-11 shows how every knee is to bow to that name - "of things in heaven, and things in earth, and things under the earth." Things in heaven refer to all the angels of God. Things in earth refer to all of mankind, whether you are a king, president, or supreme ruler or whether you are just a common man or even a beggar that lives on the street. Things under the earth refer to all the demonic forces of hell, the whole of the demonic underworld - Satan and all those with him. There is not one name or authority that can withstand the name of Jesus.

This is the name that we have taken on, the authority we have taken on. The authority of that name has been given to the church. Jesus said, "All power is given unto me in heaven and in earth " (Matthew 28:18). The Greek word here is *exousia*. So Jesus was given all authority in heaven and earth. There is no authority that was not given to Him.

Authority of the Church

Luke 9:1 says that Jesus gave the twelve apostles "power and authority over all devils, and to cure diseases." Again the Greek words used here are *dunamis* and *exousia*. Not only were they given authority to use the word against devils and diseases but they were also given the ability to demonstrate the authority that was given to them.

But the chain of authority and power did not stop there. In Ephesians 6:10, Paul urged the church to "be strong in the Lord, and in the power of his might." The Greek word behind "strong" comes from the root word *dunamis*. We are to be empowered in the Lord, demonstrating His power to all mankind. The Greek word behind "power" in this verse is *kratei*, coming from the root word *kratos*, meaning strength, might, force, and a display of might.[45]

The Greek word behind "might" in this verse is *iskus,* meaning strength, mighty power, faculty, and ability as a noun.[46] As a verb, it means to be strong, to be well, in good health, to have power, to be able, to be valid, to be of service, to be serviceable because of the ability to perform, in the condition of strength, being capable - as a strong man who is capable of lifting 500 lbs.[47] This tells us that we are first to be capable of using the Lord's power or to have it in ready service.

> We, as the church, actually have Jesus' authority at our disposal.

Next, we are to go beyond its mere ability or potential to the actual display of that might. We are to demonstrate the abilities of God. We know that God is able to do far above and beyond all that we ask or think (Ephesians 3:20). But He is able to do it according to the power that works in us. We are to allow that power to work in us. We are to demonstrate that great ability and power of God.

In talking about Jesus our Lord, Colossians 2:9-10 says that the fullness of the Godhead (including all the authority and power of the Godhead) bodily dwells in Him, who "is the head of

---

[45] "Kratos," *The Analytical Greek Lexicon Revised.*
[46] "Iskus," *ibid.*
[47] *Ibid.*

all principality and power." The Greek word behind power is *exousia* (authority). Jesus is the head or the very top or source of all authorities, regardless of their form. He has dominion over all authority. We find our completeness or fulfillment in Him, in His authority. We, as the church, have His authority at our disposal. There are guidelines in how to use it and there are limits to its accessibility to be sure, but still it has been placed in the church. It is up to us to begin to exercise it. What do we as believers have authority over?

Mark 16:17-18 lists the signs that would follow the believer. They would not just follow the apostles or certain preachers. These signs come as the result of the proper use of authority in the spiritual realm. These signs are power and authority to cast out devils, speaking with new tongues, taking up serpents, safety from poisoning (poisoning, whether of the blood or food or otherwise, is contamination), and the healing of the sick.

Taking up serpents, although definitely applicable to the physical world, may be better understood in light of Luke 10:19. In this verse, Jesus said, "Behold, I give unto you power [*exousia* - AUTHORITY] to tread on serpents and scorpions, and over all the power [*dunamis* - WORKINGS, DEMONSTRATIONS, THE EVIDENCES] of the enemy: and nothing shall by any means hurt you." Serpents and scorpions are references to the demonic forces, perhaps as certain classes or ranks or categories within hell's armies. We have authority to take up or tread on or totally destroy and exercise dominion over the attacks, the workings, the manifestations, or the displays of the powers of hell.

We are able to do this according to the power that works in us (Ephesians 3:20). This power is found in the Holy Ghost (Acts 1:8). Saucy has written, "Through life in the Spirit, the church already experiences' the powers of the age to come' (Heb 6:5, NASB)."[48] We can experience the demonstrative powers, the dynamic power, of the spiritual world that is to come through the gift of the Holy Ghost. That power is not limited to the world that is to come. We can taste of it now, even in this age.

---

[48] Robert L. Saucy, *The Church in God's Program* (Chicago: Moody Press, 1972), 87.

To illustrate the signs of the believer, I'll refer to some personal experiences. I was preaching in a church in Arizona where afterwards a man came up to me and asked me to pray for him because he felt as if he was about to be destroyed completely (going insane) from his problem. He was not able to get in touch with *any* of his emotions. He had lived for several years being absolutely void of his emotions including love, compassion, anger, grief, etc.

I began to pray for him and the Lord spoke the word "witchcraft" to my mind. I asked him if he had ever dealt with witchcraft. He responded that the aunt who raised him had been involved heavily in witchcraft. Of the three children raised by her, one was still heavily involved in witchcraft, another (his sister) was permanently locked away in a mental hospital, and the third was he, of course. He mentioned that the only thing that saved him from having to be locked up was receiving the Holy Ghost two years beforehand.

> Through an interpreter I learned that the boy was completely deaf in his left ear and had minimal hearing in his right ear.

We took authority over the evil spirits that had followed him from his childhood, bound them, and commanded them to leave. Immediately, he was delivered, got back in touch with his emotions, and gave glory to God. This demonstrates in one sense our authority over evil spirits that plague the soul of a man, our authority to "tread on serpents."

In another church about 300 miles away, I was involved in a service where God was healing everything completely and immediately. The gift of working of miracles was in operation that night. One Mexican lady who had just started to visit the church was healed of some female pains in her stomach area. This sparked her faith. She went back to her seat in the back, woke up her six-year-old son, and brought him down for prayer.

Through an interpreter I learned that the boy was completely deaf in his left ear and had minimal hearing in his right ear. I consented to pray only because I had preached the Word which stated nothing was impossible for God. Up to that point, I had never prayed for a deaf ear. I laid hands on him and asked God to please take over. He was immediately healed in both ears, was able to understand every word I said in both English and Spanish, and was able to repeat them back to me. "They shall lay hands on the sick and they shall recover."

These signs shall follow them that believe. What does it mean to believe? It is not being worried at how hard we can concentrate or thinking positive thoughts or even wondering about the amount of faith that we have. Wigglesworth noted that to believe "is to have such confidence in what the Lord said that we take Him at His word, simply because He said it."[49] The proof of believing begins with obedience.

> Our faith should surpass our emotions.

Believing is not related to feeling. Our faith should surpass our emotions. Many times I do not feel the power of electricity but I still believe in its power. I demonstrate this belief by relying on its use. When I come in contact with a situation, whether or not I feel the Holy Ghost, whether or not I feel faith, I still believe. I choose to believe. And because I believe, I depend on Him. I do not depend on my emotions or my feelings. I depend on Him because I believe in Him. I am a believer.

The Authority of God's Word

The Word of God is the highest authority. It is even higher than His name (Psalm 138:2). Our obedience to the Word of God and the principles found therein is vital to our spiritual authority. If you have something in your life that is not consistent with the Word of God, it will give the devil a foothold in your life and you will lose your authority in that area. One example is the biblical teaching on forgiving others. If we do not forgive others and harbor bitterness against others, it allows Satan to "get an advantage of us," (II Corinthians 2:9-11). In this same passage, Paul wanted to see proof of the Corinthians' obedience "in all things."

The value of obedience and submission in order to exercise control or authority over sicknesses and all the power of demonic spirits is shown in the following scriptures. The Word of God is indispensable in exercising control or authority over the devil

---

[49] Stanley Howard Frodsham, *Smith Wigglesworth: Apostle of Faith* (Springfield, MO: Gospel Publishing House, 1948), 58.

because it is the source of faith. "So then faith cometh by hearing, and hearing by the word of God," (Romans 10:17). Yet, James 1:22-25 stresses how we cannot be just hearers of the Word but must also be doers of the Word. It is only in mixing the Word of God with faith by being obedient to the Word that it becomes profitable (Hebrews 4:2). The Word of God is not profitable to us unless we learn to obey it, to be doers of the Word, and to mix it with faith, which is always demonstrated as it is backed up by works (James 2:17-18,20,26). There is no substitute to obedience to the Word of God.

Other Loopholes to Our Authority

Another example where Satan can exercise control over our lives is if we open the door through participation in witchcraft, even "white" witchcraft such as palm reading, crystal balls, hypnosis, and the horoscope. When delivering someone from demonic possession or oppression, many servants of God have found it useful to have the one being delivered to repent from the use of those forms of witchcraft.

> The attempted use of spiritual authority where you are not submitted to the will of God can result in disastrous and shameful consequences.

In addition, the attempted use of spiritual authority where you are not submitted to the will of God can result in disastrous and shameful results. The sons of Sceva were such who were not submitted to authority and tried to cast some evil spirits out of some people (Acts 19:13-20). Now, they obviously were believers. They believed by calling on the name of Jesus, the evil spirit would leave. They knew the power of people possessed with devils (they were exorcists) and would not tangle with one unless they believed they had a greater power. They were even specific enough to state to which Jesus they were referring. It was not the Jesus down the street or Jesus the tentmaker but the "Jesus whom Paul preacheth." But instead of casting the devil out, they were stripped naked and wounded. What went wrong?

Verse 13 describes them as vagabond Jews. Vagabond means "leading an unsettled or irresponsible life," and refers to wandering or "leading the life of a vagrant or tramp."[50] They were irresponsible or they refused to stay submitted under an authority. Therefore, when they tried to exercise authority themselves, the evil spirit's response was "Jesus I know, and Paul I know; but who are ye?" Jesus and Paul had the right to exercise authority but "Why do I have to listen to you when you are not under authority yourself?"

They had undermined their own authority. The result was that he jumped on them, beat them badly, and sent them running naked into the streets. Remember, also, that Paul stated that we were to be submitted to authority no only for wrath (fear of punishment) but

> A refusal to submit to authority will undermine your spiritual authority.

also for conscience sake (knowing it affects our spiritual authority).

A lack of submission to authority will also undermine one's credibility with the body of Christ. People generally are not willing to follow a loose cannon. As human beings, God created us to require some sort of order, some sort of structure. The Latter Rain Movement was one that did have a move of the Spirit but there was a problem with submission. David Pytches, a supporter of the dynamic move of the Holy Ghost, writes:

> "The Latter Rain Movement, whatever its merits, was greatly undermined by such unbridled prophetic utterances. Men and women were prophesying all kinds of words over people but were not operating under authority. Their prophecies went untested. God is not the author of confusion. There is a divine order for these things."[51]

Eventually, both the Assemblies of God and the United Pentecostal Church distanced themselves from the movement.

---

[50] "Vagabond," *The Merriam-Webster Dictionary.*

[51] David Pytches, *Some Said It Thundered* (Nashville: Oliver Nelson, 1991), 13.

In II Corinthians 10:6, Paul spoke of bringing vengeance on all disobedience (it was first found in Satan) when our obedience was fulfilled. We can judge disobedience only when we have been obedient ourselves. James 4:7 tells us that we are first to be submitted to God. Then, after we are operating properly under authority, we have the right to use the authority granted to us as a part of the Church. When we resist the devil in this manner, then he must flee from us. Otherwise, when we resist him, he feels no need to fear because we ourselves are not submitted to authority. We would have undermined our own authority. A refusal to submit to authority will undermine your spiritual authority.

CHAPTER SEVEN

SPECIFIC AUTHORITY

The question will arise as to why sometimes a healing does not take place when we pray. Do we always have authority over situations in our lives that do not meet our satisfaction? Can we change things just at our whim, if we are living in line with the principle of authority? What about things that God may be trying to use to chasten us or to develop some things in us that need perfecting?

Being obedient towards the exercise of spiritual authority also entails being sensitive to the Spirit, being led by the Spirit, and being obedient to the voice of God to do the will of God. According to I Peter 2:21, we are to follow the steps of Jesus. In Ephesians 5:1, Paul exhorts us to be "followers of God, as dear children." We are to follow God in righteousness, holiness, and godliness. This entails our actions, words, and thoughts. Yet it entails much more.

Walk in the Spirit

Galatians 5:25 says that "if we live in the spirit, let us also walk in the spirit." There is a distinction between living in the spirit and walking in the spirit. When you are born of the spirit (John 3:5) you are living in the spirit. Yet Paul made a distinction between living in the spirit and walking in the spirit. But what does walking in the spirit mean?

"Walk" comes from the Greek word *stoikeo* meaning to advance or to progress.[52] We ought to advance in our walk with God and the ways of the spirit. It also means to frame one's conduct by a certain rule.[53] In the context where this verse is found, this meaning is seen clearly. Our lives ought to bear the fruit of walking or advancing in the spirit. But that is beyond the scope of this study. The point I want to look at here is that which focuses on advancing or progressing in the ways of the spirit.

Spiritual Growth

In regards to advancing or progressing in the spirit, the concept of growth is seen as necessary in the spirit realm. Growth is one of the strongest principles found in the universe. Everything that lives must grow and develop. Seeds grow into plants. Puppies grow into dogs. Kittens grow into cats. Babies grow into adults. There are numerous other things in our physical world that must grow in order to survive. Fires typically must grow or die.

I have heard it said by those who have studied trees that as long as the tree is growing (whether by developing its root structure, putting out new branches and leaves, growing flowers, producing fruit, reaching for higher heights, or going for deeper depths) it will be fine. But when the tree stops

> When we stop growing spiritually, we begin to die.

growing, it begins dying. According to some scientists, even the universe is continuing to expand. Growth is necessary to the continued existence and long-term survival of living things. Life is at its strongest in a human being as long as that human being is growing (developing positively – which is differentiated from getting fat). But when we stop growing and developing, old age begins to creep in.

---

[52] "Stoikeo," *The Analytical Greek Lexicon Revised.*
[53] *Ibid.*

In like manner, in our spiritual life, we must always be growing. We can grow in the quality of our communion with God, in our knowledge of the Word, and in knowledge of the truth. We can increase in understanding and in wisdom. We can expand our understanding of truth, our love for God and others, and our purity. We should grow in the fruit of the spirit and in the gifts of the spirit evident in our lives. We should increase in faith. We must develop our character and grow in our honesty with God and ourselves. We can grow in power with God. The point is that we must be growing somehow. When we stop growing spiritually, we begin to die. Old age or complacency begins to set in and we find ourselves stalemated and in the condition of the Laodicean Church.

We will recognize there are stages of growth in our walk with God also. In discussing the Kingdom of God, Jesus stated that it is like a seed that grows (Mark 4:28). It has "first the blade, then the ear, after that the full corn in the ear." A human being grows from being in the mother's womb, to infant, to a babe beginning to walk, to a young child, to a growing boy, to an adolescent, to a mature adult. Likewise, there are stages of growth in the spirit realm. The daily exercise of the power of God should grow "from strength to strength".

So we must walk in the spirit. By "walking in the spirit" I am not referring to something spooky or something involving an ungodly mysticism. I am simply referring to allowing God to have complete control over our lives, being submitted to Him, and letting His grace have its desired effect in our lives.

We must walk in the spirit. We must progress, advance, and move forward in the areas of the spirit. If we will walk in the spirit (grow or advance in it), we will not fulfill the lusts of the flesh (Galatians 5:16). It does not mean that we will never fall, but that the lusts of the flesh will not have their complete work of destruction in our lives. The lusts of our flesh will not be fulfilled in us. The Greek root word behind "fulfill" is *teleo*, which refers to the lusts finding their complete work in us,[54] i.e., it would not finish its course in bringing us to sin and ultimately being destroyed (James 1:15).

---

[54] "Teleo," *The Analytical Greek Lexicon Revised.*

Becoming Sons of God

John 1:12 says, "But as many as received him, to them gave he power to become the sons of God, even to them that believe on his name." The Greek word behind "power" is *exousia*, which refers to authority rather than the display of energy. Those who received Jesus Christ have been given the authority to become the sons of God. The word "become" speaks of a process, a motion of growth. We are given the authority to be in the position of becoming a son of God. What is left is the actual working out of it in our lives. As Dr. Dan Segraves says, "We begin to become what we are."

Romans 8:14 says, "For as many as are led by the spirit of God, they are the sons of God." The actual manifestation of being the sons of God is that we are led by His Spirit or guided by His Spirit. We are not out to use this great power that God has given to us as we would desire it (which would often be to satisfy our own lusts) but as God desires it to be used. James specified that we can ask without receiving if we are asking amiss, that we may consume it upon our lusts (James 4:3). It is not our will but His will that is to be performed.

This is why we need to develop a sensitive ear to hear what the Spirit is saying. We need to learn what God is trying to accomplish in a certain situation and then work in harmony with it. We do not prophesy just to say what we wish to happen but to show what God is going to perform. Jesus was led by the Spirit when He only healed one man and bypassed many others (John 5:1-9).

When the Spirit is leading us, it is like power that is brought under control. It is no longer lightning that strikes randomly from the sky but electricity that is channeled to light up a city at night. Power that is out of control can be very destructive, while power under control can be very constructive and edifying.

When you are led, you are headed in a certain direction. When we are led by the Spirit, we are already walking in the spirit. We have power that we can exercise. But it is under the control of the Spirit.

Those who are led by the Spirit of God are the sons of God. It is no longer simply an authority to become a son of God, as is the case when we receive Christ. We are now acting out the part.

Being led by the Spirit means being in touch with what God is saying. I was praying before a particular service where I was holding a revival and I asked God exactly what He wanted to do as far as miracles were concerned. He spoke to me that someone would come to be prayed for with pain in their hands and that they would be healed. It was nothing major or profound. But I was put on alert.

Sure enough, at the end of the service, a lady (named Sister Vazis – a professor at the University of Arizona) came to be prayed for. She had crippling arthritis and was having tremendous pain in her hands. I told her what God had spoken to me and we prayed. Immediately, the pain left and did not return. In fact, the next day she was scheduled to move out of her home and she did all the packing by herself all day long without any pain or hindrance. The miraculous result was simply the product of following the leading of God's Spirit.

Hearing the voice of God is not limited to details of physical conditions. Once, while working in the altar service in the same church, God spoke to me about a young lady whom I had never met before (I later learned her name was Sister Martin). He wanted me to tell her that God was going to take care of her job situation and would fight her battles for her. What I found out the next night shocked me.

She worked for the Arizona Department of Public Safety, Arizona's police department. To keep it short, she had been receiving persecution from her boss (seemingly directed towards her religion) and was in danger of losing her job. She was worrying so much about it that she was not far from a nervous breakdown. But the message from God spoke peace to her heart. She went to work the next day relaxed.

Within the next week, the situation had so reversed itself that she had been called up to headquarters in Phoenix to review the situation with her supervisor's boss. The last I heard, her supervisor was the one in danger of losing her job if she did not straighten up. God had worked things out. He had fought the battle. The glory belongs to God, but there would never have been the peace if someone did not hear God's voice in the situation.

Being in Touch with the Spirit of Life

The natural body works in natural reaction to the head, the brain. It works as "second nature," performing the desires of the head. In reading a study about the complexity of the human brain, the author analyzed a quarterback backing up and throwing a pass. He said that it would take some of our modern computers a much longer time to do certain calculations than it does for the human brain to do them. The quarterback must back up while holding on to the ball and being aware of the efforts of opposing linemen who are trying to tackle him, having to move around if they come too close. He must apply the right pressure in holding on to the ball to keep it from dropping. He must also keep track of two or three receivers going downfield and running their patterns while the defenders try to interfere with the play.

> We can only fulfill the will of the Father to the extent that we have taken on the mind of Christ.

After selecting the receiver to catch the pass, he must then calculate how far the receiver is, how fast they are running, and the force with which to throw the ball to cover the distance. He must figure out the angle at which he must throw the ball so that it minimizes the opportunity for someone on the opposing team to interfere with the play. He must time it so that the receiver and the ball arrive at the same place simultaneously since the receiver is running. He must calculate the precise moment to release the ball while allowing it to roll off his fingertips so that it will spiral and become easier to catch for the receiver. He must take into account all outside elements that may interfere with any of the calculations he has made such as the wind. Our mind does all of the calculations in a split second. It is not concentrating hard on the calculations. It just thinks in that general direction and the body automatically follows through with the mind's desires.

The body of Christ ought to work the same way. As God thinks in a certain direction, we ought to be sensitive enough to naturally follow through with doing His will. This applies to miracles as well as all the operation of all the gifts of the spirit and doing what is right and good and wise in any given situation. This is why we must put on the mind of Christ (I Corinthians 2:16, Philippians 2:5).

"Lord, help us to put on the mind of Christ. Help us to be so finely tuned in to what You desire to do that it becomes like second nature to be led by your Spirit. In Jesus' name."

According to I Peter 4:1, we ought to be armed with the mind of Christ so that we do not live to fulfill the lusts of men but the will of God. We can only fulfill the will of the Father to the extent that we have taken on the mind of Christ. We can only do His will while being sensitive to His Spirit and hearing His voice.

We should be so finely tuned in to the mind of God that He needs only to think in a certain direction so that we will automatically follow through on it. Peter, on impulse, almost by natural reaction, commanded the lame man to rise and walk in Acts 3. We must be bold enough to step out and be a follower of God in every situation. This is what will bring Him great glory.

Results of Being Led by the Spirit

In Luke 4:1, we read that Jesus was led by the Spirit into the wilderness. In Luke 4:14, we read that "Jesus returned in the power of the Spirit into Galilee." Exercising the power of the Spirit is the direct result of being led by the Spirit. The Greek root word behind "power" in this verse is *dunamis*. This refers not just to an authority to use a certain ability but the actual demonstration of that power, strength, that which produces results, might, a manifestation or instance of power, energy on display (as seen in the explosion of dynamite), external power, a show of force.[55]

In Jesus' ministry afterward, the power of the Spirit was continually demonstrated to deliver people. As we saw in Chapter One, the gospels are filled

> Exercising the power of the Spirit is the direct result of being led by the Spirit.

with accounts of Him healing the sick, cleansing the lepers, opening the blinded eyes, unstopping deaf ears, stretching withered limbs, making the lame to walk and the dumb to talk, raising the dead, casting out devils, etc. In fact, John 21:25 says that if everything was written about what Jesus did, the Apostle John didn't know if even the whole world could hold the books that would have to be written.

---

[55] "Dunamis," *The Analytical Greek Lexicon Revised.*

Following the Spirit

In John 14:12, Jesus said, "He that believeth on me, the works that I do shall he do also; and greater works than these shall he do." We often read this verse as if it said "the works that I **did** shall he do also." Actually, it reads "the works that I **do** shall he do also." The words "I do" in this verse come from the Greek words *ego poio,* which is found in the present tense, indicative mood, active voice. This refers to on-going action. "The present tense indicates *progressive* action at the *present* – 'he is loosing.'"[56]

Perhaps it is best to see what Jesus meant by referring to another passage of Scripture, John 5:17, 19-20, 36. In this story, Jesus had healed a lame man at the pool of Bethesda. Unfortunately, some religious leaders became upset because He did it on the Sabbath. So they questioned Him.

First of all, Jesus replied that He was able to do nothing of Himself as a man. The miracles that took place resulted from His following what the Father showed Him. As the Son can do nothing of Himself, so we can do nothing by ourselves. We can only do that which the Father is doing. We can only do in the natural that which God is doing in the spiritual world.

We must be sensitive enough to look into the spirit world and find out what God is doing, hearing the voice of God, being in tune with His Spirit. We have no ability within ourselves to work great miracles, to perform a spiritual work in someone's life, or to see the supernatural brought into reality. Our holiness will never be good enough.

> Jesus showed us what happens when a person is led by the Spirit of God.

Our own righteousness will never earn it for us. Our works from our flesh will accomplish nothing. We can do absolutely nothing by ourselves. We must depend on God to lead us first and to work the miracle as we follow Him.

Jesus then stated that He worked only in the direction that the Father worked, stating "The Son can do nothing of Himself, but what He seeth the Father do: for what things soever He doeth, these also doeth the Son likewise." Jesus had told them, in

[56] Ray Summers, *Essentials of New Testament Greek* (Nashville, TN: Broadman Press, 1950), 11.

essence, that "the Father is working hitherto (in this direction) and I work or follow in the same steps" (verse 17). Jesus looked into the spirit realm, found out what was the will of God, and worked in that direction. Jesus was showing us what happens when the Spirit of God leads a person.

This is why God backed Him up by working the miracles. Jesus was simply laying out an example of what we should do in our personal ministries, so that we would be able to follow in His steps. This is what is meant by John 14:12, "the works that I do shall he do also." We must follow what Jesus Christ is doing at the present moment in the spiritual realm. What Jesus saw the Father do, which He knew because He sought the will of God (verse 30), He followed in obedience.

This is the same way that believers are to follow the voice of the Spirit. We must seek to know the will of God so that we can know in which direction He is moving and follow His Spirit. The way we know the will of God is by spending time in prayer and reading His Word and by submitting our will entirely to Him. We know what God desires to do by seeking His will.

The Spirit also Follows Us

The teaching that the Spirit follows us as well is seen in Matthew 16:17-19. Jesus stated that He would *build* His church on the rock of the revelation of truth and that the gates of hell (symbolizing the strongest defenses of all the forces of hell; their last line of defense; their highest authorities, devices, and plans) would not withstand it. Any group or organization that is *built* contains within it a structure of authority.

Jesus then says, "Whatsoever thou shalt bind on earth shall be bound in heaven: and whatsoever thou shalt loose on earth shall be loosed in heaven." Here, "heaven" refers to the spiritual world, which rules over the natural world.[57] "Earth" is a reference to the physical world that we live in, the natural world. Keep in mind that authority is always witnessed in a communication of some sort, usually in the form of a word (whether spoken or written). The promise to the church is that whatever we would bind in earth (the natural realm) with our words, God would reach

---

[57] For more on how this works, read Part I of my book, *The High Places* (Roanoke, VA: Spirit of Life Press, 1999).

into the heavens (the spiritual realm) and bind its effectiveness there. Whatever we will loose in earth (the natural realm) with our words, God will reach into heaven (the spiritual realm) and loose it there or release it so that it may become effective in our lives.

It is the principle of authority in action. It is the demonstrated power backing up the authority. It is the display of the energy that is symbolized by the spoken word. It is the *exousia* being supported by the *dunamis*. We can bind a sickness, disease, affliction, infirmity, or evil spirit. We can loose an individual, release faith, peace, even finances. We can bring peace to a troubled mind or unwind a situation. It is all proof of God honoring the authority that He has placed in the church. It is the Lord working to confirm the word (Mark 16:20).

> What we believe is just as important as the fact that we believe.

If we believe on Jesus according to the scripture, the works that He is doing at the moment we will do as well as we follow in obedience. Believing is not simply affirming His existence or simple mental assent. There is a reference to full persuasion, being fully convinced. As Smith Wigglesworth said, "Because you dare to believe, you act in obedience."[58] If we believe, we will obey. What we believe is just as important as the fact that we believe. In this passage (John 14:12-14), what we believe is also mentioned. We must believe that Jesus and the Father are one (John 14:9-11).

When we go through the exercise of believing, and specifically believing the right thing, we go to the next step – being led by the Spirit. Verse 12 of John 14 is a direct reference to being sensitive to the Spirit. As the Holy Spirit moves in a certain direction, we are to follow His lead. What we see God working in the spiritual world, we follow through in obedience in the natural world. The result is greater works than those that were performed by Jesus up until that time.

> When Jesus referred to works, He often had the miraculous in mind.

---

[58] Frodsham, 112.

The Works Jesus Did

What works were performed by Jesus? To what works was Jesus referring? When John the Baptist was sitting in prison discouraged, he sent messengers to Jesus to affirm whether Jesus was the Messiah or not (Matthew 11:2-6). Jesus' response was "Go and shew John again those things which ye do hear and see: The blind receive their sight, and the lame walk, the lepers are cleansed, and the deaf hear, the dead are raised up, and the poor have the gospel preached to them." In Luke's account of this event, he recorded that in the same hour, Jesus had performed many miracles (Luke 7:21). These are among the things we will do when we are sensitive to and obedient to the moving of the Spirit of God.

When Jesus referred to works, He often had the miraculous in mind. When He told people to believe Him for the works' sake, He had the miraculous in mind (John 10:37-38). When He referred to mighty works being done in Chorazin, Bethsaida, and Capernaum, He was referring to the miraculous. When He told us to let our light shine so that men may see our good works and glorify God, He had the miraculous in mind. He wants us to do the same works – yes, even greater works.

Working with God

I Corinthians 3:9 says that we are laborers together with God. We are not just to work for God; we are to work with Him. What we see Him doing, we work in obedience. We are to do the same thing. We are to work in that direction, following Him, letting Him confirm the Word. We must give God a part in our evangelistic effort. Greater yet, it should be stated that we should become a part of His evangelistic effort. Let us follow the leading of His Spirit. Let us be led by the Spirit.

There is nothing wrong with knocking on ten thousand doors and witnessing, but it would be much more profitable if we would follow the leading of the Spirit. This does not give us the excuse for being lazy in outreach. We still must do our part. The question is: whom is God dealing with? Let us work in harmony with the supernatural world.

I recently heard the story of a town in Canada which had seen many ministers come and go while trying to start a church there without any of them having much success. Finally, an old missionary went there who was not even able to speak the dominant language – French. We supported him for one year while he built the church no one else could build.

How did he do it? He would drive around the city waiting for the Holy Ghost to quicken him. When God would point out a certain soul to him, he would go and witness to that person in whatever manner the Holy Ghost was leading him and lead that soul to Jesus Christ. Miracles would happen and souls would be won. By the end of the first year, he had built a church of about 200

> When you are imitating God so much that you are talking like Him, thinking like Him, and acting like Him, the devil becomes very afraid because there is nothing he can do against you.

people. He was simply being led by the Holy Ghost and the Lord worked with him, confirming the word.

Mark 16:20 says that the Lord worked with the apostles, confirming the word with signs following. The miracles happened because they followed God. There is almost a Holy Ghost "choo-choo" train in effect here. First, we follow God. Then the signs follow us as we believe (and obey). The sinners follow the signs that point them to Jesus Christ. This results in revival and growth.

Imitating God

In John 10:27, Jesus states that "My sheep hear my voice, and I know them, and they follow me." The Greek root word behind "follow" is *akoloutheo*. It means literally "to imitate."[59] Jesus' sheep hear His voice and follow or imitate Him. In Ephesians 5:1, Paul entreats us to be followers of God. He uses the same Greek root word showing us to be imitators of God.

What does imitating God mean? Does being in His service constitute imitating God? In John 12:26, Jesus says, "If any man serve me, let him follow me." There is a marked distinction between simply serving God and being an imitator of God. Many

---

[59] "Akoloutheo," *The Analytical Greek Lexicon Revised.*

are involved in the service of God (even in "the ministry") but are not imitators of God.

I believe that imitating God is best illustrated by the discussion in I Corinthians 12-14, the fruit of the Spirit mentioned in Galatians 5:22-23, and the life of Jesus Christ. I Corinthians 12-14 discusses the operation of the gifts of the spirit. One individual has classified them as follows. The word of wisdom, the word of knowledge, and the discerning of spirits are known as the mental gifts. These gifts help you to think like God. The gift of prophecy, divers kinds of tongues, and the interpretation of tongues are known as the vocal gifts. These help you to talk like God. The gifts of healing, the gift of faith, and the working of miracles are known as the power gifts. These help you to act like God.

> Our call to repentance is also a call to allow God to help us.

When you are thinking like God, talking like God, and acting like God, then James 4:7 comes into play. You are submitted to God and you represent God. So when the devil sees you coming, he sees God coming and runs the other way. You can resist him and he will flee.

In Matthew 4:18-19, Jesus told Peter to "follow me." This was Peter's first day with Jesus. The Greek word behind "follow" means to "come after me." Jesus was asking Peter to leave what he was doing and to come after Him. This was Peter's call to repentance. God's first call to the world has always been to "come after me," to repent from running away from Him. We run from God because of sin in our lives. Instinctively, we know God's holiness cannot tolerate sin. We run because we instinctively know the penalty for sin – death.

In Luke's account of the story (Luke 5:1-11) Peter had the same impulse to run away from God. Only he expressed it by telling Jesus to "Depart from me." What was Peter's reason for wanting to get away from Jesus? Who would tell Jesus to "Get away from me." Peter had a very common reason: "I am a sinful man, O Lord."

It has been said that sin produces a great gulf between God and us. In reality, sin not only produces a great gulf between God and us, it also places us on a course running away from God. But God's call is for us to repent. He calls for us to quit running away from Him and, instead, come toward Him. He wants us to seek Him, to pursue Him, to seek Him with all our heart and soul. He is a rewarder of those who diligently seek Him (Hebrews 11:6).

He cannot help us if we are running away from Him. So He sends His message for us to repent, to turn toward Him. We run away from Him because we feel condemned as a result of the sentence of death in our lives. The sentence of death comes from sin because the wages of sin is death (Romans 6:23) and the soul that sins shall die (Ezekiel 18:4, 20).

But Jesus stated that "God sent not His Son into the world to condemn the world; but that the world through Him might be saved" (John 3:17). Jesus came to help man, to seek and to save that which was lost, to redeem man from his worthless state. So He calls us to repentance. He calls us to quit running away from God and start pursuing Him. Actually, our call to repentance is a call to allow God to help us.

Jesus wanted Peter to come after Him. So Peter forsook his nets and came after Jesus. But Jesus did not stop there. Peter followed Jesus for three and a half years. After that, Jesus was crucified, buried, and then He proceeded to rise again the third day. In John 21, we have the last recorded conversation between Jesus and Peter. Three times Jesus asks Peter if he loves Him. Each time Peter's response is in the affirmative. Jesus then tells Peter to feed His sheep.

Jesus sees that Peter does not get the point. The book of John repeatedly refers to Jesus as the good Shepherd, the Shepherd that gives His life for the sheep, the Door to the sheepfold, etc. A good shepherd feeds his sheep. He ministers to his sheep. Jesus wanted Peter to be like Him. But Peter wasn't getting it.

Jesus went on to remind him how that when he was young, he girded himself and went pretty much wherever he wanted to go. In other words, he was led by his own will or by his own spirit. But Jesus said that the time would come when he would not do what he wanted to do. Another would gird him and another would carry him. He would no longer be led by his own will. He would be led by someone else's will. He would be led by another spirit. He even gave an example of how this would be evidenced. Jesus stated that "thou shalt stretch forth thy hands" – a reference to the kind of death that Peter would some day willingly die (definitely not in line with Peter's will).

When Jesus had made this statement, He then told Peter, "Follow me." Jesus' first command for Peter's life and his last

> God calls us to imitate Him. In essence, we are called to be led by His Spirit.

command for Peter's life were so similar. "Follow me." But whereas the first time Jesus used a phrase meaning "come after me," this time He used the Greek root word *akoloutheo*, meaning to "imitate me." In essence, Jesus was saying, "Peter, do the works that I do. Say the things that I say. Think like I think. Peter, be like me." Whew! That was a tall order. No wonder Peter wanted to find out what Jesus was requiring of the Apostle John.

Jesus was calling Peter to learn to be led by the Spirit, rather than ruled by his flesh. He was challenging Peter to be led by the Holy Spirit of God rather than his fleshly desires. "Follow me – Imitate me. Do it like I do it. Live like I do. Be like me." So God calls us to imitate Him.

Following Wind

How do you follow or imitate God? In answer to this question, a set of rules is often what we desire. It's what we often think is needed. We look for something that we can measure up to on an outward appearance in attire or ritual act or word. But to imitate Jesus does not mean we must fulfill all the requirements of a certain rigid code. Rather, it is done through following His Spirit. It is "not by might, nor by power, but by My Spirit" (Zechariah 4:6).

We are often repulsed (in our flesh) to following after the Spirit because it is not limited to a certain set of actions that we can follow or a code that we can live up to that satisfies that parameters of following after the Spirit. Rather it is a continual course of following directions. The flesh loses total control. We end up decreasing while He ends up increasing. We would rather that what is required of us would be a single, one time accomplishment or action instead of constantly following instructions. We would much rather rely on ourselves than to depend on another.

Following God's Spirit often seems hard to us – like understanding wind. We can hear the wind blowing and can ascertain its present direction but cannot tell where it will end up. It's hard to go outside and start running after the wind. How do you follow it? It's the same thing with following the Spirit of God.

Sometimes we know that God is moving, perhaps even what He is telling us to say or do, but cannot see what the result will be. We are forced to step out in faith, believing that God will not embarrass us. We must learn to see, hear, and understand God's ways.

Concerning knowing what God is saying, only time spent with God can help you learn His voice. Just as you can tell a friend's voice because you have spent so much time communicating with him or her, so you can learn God's voice by communicating with Him. Spend time in prayer and the reading of His word. The voice of God will not contradict the written word of God. Knowing God's voice can be like learning the taste of bacon. Once you know it, it may be difficult to describe its taste but you will know what it is if you taste it again. So it is with knowing the voice of God in a certain matter.

God is looking for those who will believe, who are longing for a demonstration of His Spirit among men. He is searching for those who desire to become sensitive to the Spirit, to know the voice of the Lord, to become imitators of God.

"Lord, anoint my eyes with eyesalve that I may see the things of the spirit. Anoint my ears that I may hear what your Spirit is saying. Anoint my mind that I may understand the things you show me. Anoint my heart to receive it exactly as you would have me to receive it, and anoint *me* to respond in faith and in obedience as you would have me to respond. Help me to obey, imitate, follow you."

To follow someone or to imitate him or her, you must have your focus on him or her. You must turn your eyes on them. You must "turn your eyes upon Jesus." Then we can "look full into His wonderful face. And the things of the world will grow strangely dim, in the light of His glory and grace." If your eyes are on God, you will see the glory of God, as did Stephen. That glory will outshine the things of this world.

Faith comes into the picture in that it is demonstrated by simple obedience. We "come after" God to "imitate" Him. Paul said to be followers or imitators of God as dear children (Ephesians 5:1). We imitate Him as children imitate their parents. When we imitate Him, we are demonstrating obedience and exercising faith. And faith is the key that opens the door to all the gifts of the Spirit. Faith is the key to seeing the signs, wonders, and miracles that the early church saw and that helps to bring wonderful God-led revival. Let us be "followers of God." Let us be imitators of God. When the Spirit leads us, we do whatever the Spirit is doing. We then become true imitators of God.

CHAPTER EIGHT

RELATION TO FAITH

In Mark 11:22, Jesus said, "Have faith in God." Here we find faith more closely tied to spiritually authority. We must first come to the conclusion that our faith is not primarily and ultimately in medicine and doctors. Our faith is not in advanced psychology. For safety sake, my faith is not rooted in the best security systems. My faith is not in my bank account (thank God). I do not base my faith in a drug rehabilitation program, Alcoholics Anonymous, or some other social program to change our world. I am not against these things but my faith is not founded in them. My faith is not in a particular politician or social leader. My faith is in God.

When I run into a problem, I do not first look in a medical journal for my answer. I do not go first digging in a psychology textbook for the answers to our modern problems. I do not look for solutions in a column in the daily newspaper or some other media personality. I look in the Word of God. My faith is in God.

Our faith is to be in God. We are not to limit our faith to the power of positive thinking. I am not against positive thinking because faith does not grow well in a negative atmosphere. But our faith is not to be restricted to the principles of positive thinking. We are not to have faith in how hard we can concentrate in making the pain go away. Miracles are not based on how hard we can concentrate. If your faith is simply in mental powers, you are tampering with some psychic spirit. This is not biblical Christianity.

The truth is that we are not even to place our faith in the concept of faith. It is not a matter of how much faith we have. It is not a question of how strong our faith is. It is a matter of placing our faith, our trust, and our confidence in God. It means placing our complete assurance, our dependence, and our hope in God. We place it in His ability, in His power, in what He can do. We rely on Him, not ourselves.

> The mountain is under no obligation to move until we speak to it. Until we exercise our authority that mountain will not move.

We do not rely on our own faith to accomplish the act. We do not rely on our own authority, our own power, or our own abilities. We do not depend on our own holiness or righteousness or our works to be the source of our miracle. We trust in who God is. That is when things must happen. God may not always respond to need but He will respond to faith that is in Him.

Then the promises of the next verses spring into action. "Whosoever shall say unto this mountain, Be thou removed, and be thou cast into the sea; and shall not doubt in his heart, but shall believe that those things which he saith shall come to pass; he shall have whatsoever he saith." If our faith is founded in God, then we can speak to the mountain and it must obey.

Notice that we must speak to the mountain. The mountain is under no obligation to move until we speak to it. Until we exercise our authority that mountain will not move. Remember that authority is always manifested in a communication, usually a word (spoken or written). If we do speak, and if we believe that we will receive that which we have spoken, then we will possess that which we have spoken. It is on these premises that we can receive that which we pray for (Mark 11:24). We must believe. If we do not ask in faith, James said, "Let not that man think that he shall receive any thing from the Lord" (James 1:7).

In Matthew 17:20, Jesus took this a step further when He said, "If ye have faith as a grain of mustard seed, ye shall say unto this mountain, Remove hence to yonder place; and it shall remove;

and nothing shall be impossible unto you." There are no impossibilities when you are following the Spirit of God in obedience while seeking His will and placing your faith in God. This is the principle of spiritual authority.

"In My Name"

Jesus also stated, "Whatsoever ye shall ask in my name, that will I do, that the Father may be glorified in the Son. If ye shall ask anything in my name, I will do it" (John 14:13-14). This does not mean that we need only verbalize the name of Jesus. There is no magic in simply pronouncing the name of Jesus. If that were the case, the question could rise as to which pronunciation would be correct, to make sure the "formula" was right. The name of Jesus is pronounced differently in every language.

It is not the way that you phonetically pronounce His name that matters. It is not a magical phrase. We are not practicing some Biblical form of voodoo or a Christian brand of witchcraft. For sure, we are to include the mentioning of the name of Jesus, but it goes beyond simple vocalization. Peter told how a miracle took place because of "his name through faith in his name" (Acts 3:16). Biblical faith must be active in the releasing of the name of Jesus.

When the Bible speaks of someone's name, it encompasses the totality of the person, including their authority, their power, and even their person. The idea is that we must walk in His authority, in His stead, in His person, in the place of Jesus Christ on earth. This is how we operate in His name. If we will ask in His name, coming to God not in our name (our own authority, righteousness, works, or holiness) but in the stead of His son Jesus Christ, we will have that which we have asked. The Apostle John stated that if we asked anything according to His will, then God would hear us. And if we know that God hears us on a matter, then we know that we automatically have our petition granted to us.

However, we must always remember that there are some things that Jesus would not have prayed for. James taught us that there were some things we would not receive even if we asked for it, if we asked outside of the will of God for something we would use to consume on our lusts. Jesus prayed in the will of God. So we who are involved in the work of God must operate in the name of Jesus, in the person of Jesus Christ. We must operate in His authority, doing His will.

Smith Wigglesworth wrote, "The Lord would have us to be walking epistles of His word. Jesus is the Word and is the power in us, and it is His desire to work in and through us His own good pleasure. We must believe that He is in us."[60] This is how we become truly usable instruments in the hands of God. Smith Wigglesworth also noted, "I find that in all my Lord did He said that He did not do it, but that another in Him did the work. What a holy submission!" [61] To gain spiritual authority, one must also be submitted to the promptings of the Holy Ghost, obeying the fresh voice of God. It goes back to recognizing God's authority in our lives and submitting to it.

The Centurion's Faith

The centurion may not have understood all the intricacies that involve spiritual authority. This may be why he could not use it himself. However, he knew enough about how authority worked in the natural world to know that Jesus had the same type of authority and power over every type of sickness or disease. Even for us New Testament Christians, it is impossible to understand spiritual authority by our own understanding. "The natural man receiveth not the things of the Spirit of God: for they are foolishness unto him: neither can he know them, because they are spiritually discerned" (I Corinthians 2:14).

In writing about the spiritual authority of the church, Hagin states, "You never will understand the authority of the believer only with your intellect; you must get the spiritual revelation out of it."[62] You must understand spiritual authority through the lens of faith to get the spiritual revelation. You need to receive it with your spirit.

---

[60] Smith Wigglesworth, *Ever Increasing Faith* (Springfield, MO: Gospel Publishing House, 1924), 82.

[61] *Ibid.,* 142.

[62] Kenneth Hagin, *The Believer's Authority* (Tulsa, OK: Faith Library Publications, 1984), 13.

Faith Must Outweigh the Circumstances

We must also remember that regardless of what the situations may say, the Word of God is true and our faith must be based on it. Our faith must not be based on the evidence or the situations. The Word teaches that when God (or His authority) speaks, it must be obeyed, even if it involves the creation of the world to accomplish it. So it is with all those who exercise spiritual authority correctly.

In the scientific world, facts must control every belief, theory, hypothesis, and presupposition. But in the supernatural realm this is not the case. In the spiritual world, faith must control the facts. This is true because you are not just trying to increase knowledge or learn information as in the physical world of science. You are working to change situations, to determine destinies, to exercise authority, to demonstrate the power of God. Let your faith outweigh the circumstances.

I believe God is a rewarder of those that diligently seek Him. If we will seek Him with our whole heart, stepping out in faith, He will answer and confirm His Word. I was in a church where, while everyone was leaving the church after a Sunday morning service, I found out there was a lady who, among other things, had burrs in each of her heels. This caused tremendous pain when any pressure was put on it. This made it virtually impossible for her to walk. She would manage about ten steps with a cane before she would have to stop because of the intensity of the pain.

In my youthful impulsiveness (described this way for the benefit of those who may not understand a choice to exercise faith), I told her that I wanted to pray for her that evening at the close of the service. I didn't know it then but that statement sparked her faith. In that evening service, God completely healed her. She was able to stand, walk, and even stomp on her feet with no pain. The next day she decided to go for a walk around the block with no cane and received no pain. I believe that God simply rewarded a young minister who was willing to step out and give God an opportunity to work and also rewarded a woman who was willing to believe that it was her night for a miracle. God will honor faith anywhere He finds it.

I have run into cases where it seemed like I was the only one who believed. In one church, I remember telling the congregation at the close of the service that God was about to perform some miracles. Out of the corner of my eye I saw the pastor immediately bury his head into his hands as he doubted that God really would do anything. He probably wondered, "How could this young man make such a foolish statement?"

That night God healed a woman of her eyesight. She was legally blind, wore thick prescription glasses, and could not see six-inch letters only twenty feet away. By the time service was over, she was able to see the fine second hand on a face-sized clock on the back of the wall of the church while standing at the front of the church. She had been in that

> Perhaps only she and I believed at the first that it could happen, but everyone was a believer after the miracle – even the pastor.

prior condition for twelve years and had been prayed for many times before but without a miracle taking place.

When she saw that she was completely healed, she ran back to her pew and grabbed her purse. She ran back to the altar area in the front, took her glasses out of her purse, and tore them up in front of the congregation. Perhaps only she and I believed at the first that it could happen but everyone was a believer after the miracle – even the pastor. Seven months later I heard from the pastor that she still had her miracle and could see well. God will honor faith when He finds it, even if everyone else is doubting. Let your faith outweigh the circumstances.

If we understand that our authority is higher than the situation we are encountering (whether evil spirits, sickness, disease), then we have confidence that the commands issued in the name of Jesus (His authority and power) will be accomplished. Our faith works in spite of the view of present circumstances. The mountain must be moved. In talking about faith that contradicts the circumstances, Hagin carries it so far as to say,

> "Faith is involved in exercising spiritual
> authority. Yes, there are times when evil spirits
> come out immediately, but if they don't when you

speak the word of faith, don't get disturbed about
it.

"I base my faith on what the Word says.
Some people's faith is not based on the Bible,
however, it's based on a manifestation. They
operate outside faith in the sense realm. If they get
certain manifestations, they think the devil's
gone....

"As Smith Wigglesworth often said, 'I'm
not moved by what I see. I'm not moved by what I
feel. I'm moved only by what I believe.'"[63]

Indeed, the following story is related about Wigglesworth
and his convictions about operating in the authority of Jesus
Christ.

"He was called to pray in Kansas City for
a demon-possessed woman. When he reached the
home the demon power in the woman was most
violent in its curses. He commanded the evil
spirits in the name of Jesus to depart. He then
prepared to leave the home. All the way that he
walked to the door the woman followed him, and
from her mouth there poured out a tremendous
volume of curses. He did not say, 'I guess I did
not pray the prayer of faith; I had better go back
and pray again.' To him such a course would have
been failure. He turned and spoke to the demon
power in that woman with authority saying, 'I told
you to leave.' That was enough. The woman was
completely delivered and her pastor stated later
that she had no recurrence of demon
possession."[64]

Once again, let your faith outweigh the circumstances. Tie
your faith to the unchanging Word of God.

---

[63] *Ibid.,* 24
[64] Frodsham, 62.

Faith Is Not Related to Feeling

Authority is a fact. It is not a feeling, nor is it subject to circumstances. God has already placed us in heavenly places in the same seat as Christ (Ephesians 2:5-6). We are placed in the same position of authority. In this passage, Jesus had already been placed in heavenly places by the right hand of God (the right hand of God is symbolic of His power and authority). He was placed "Far above all principality, and power, and might, and dominion [each describing different areas of authority], and every name that is named [every authority that is found], not only in this world, but also in that which is to come" (Ephesians 1:20-21, comments within brackets are mine).

The passage goes on to show how all this was placed under His feet (a symbol of His conquering all their authority and of their submission to Him) and how He is the head over all things to the church, His body. It interesting to note that the lowest part of the body (the feet, the "weakest" or lowest member in the church) is still over all the authorities mentioned in these two verses.

In reference to Mark 16:17-18, Hagin expresses it like this: "That authority is yours whether you feel like you've got it or not. Authority has nothing to

> Authority is a fact. It is not a feeling, nor is it subject to circumstances.

do with feelings. But you must exercise it."[65] Do not let your faith be tied to your feelings because then your faith will be forced to falter when your feelings are not strong. Tie your faith to the Word of God and your faith will not need to waver. Heaven and earth (this whole universe) may pass away but the Word of God shall never pass away (Matthew 24:35, Mark 13:31). It has been forever established in heaven (Psalm 119:89, 152). It will not change. Connect your faith with the Word of God.

Hagin also notes the principle of being sensitive to God's Spirit in exercising spiritual authority. "We know from the Word that we have spiritual authority, but we must depend upon the Holy Spirit to help us in ministering authority."[66] If all of us who are involved in the work of evangelism (at home and abroad)

---

[65] Hagin, 34.
[66] *Ibid.*, 60.

would begin to exercise the spiritual authority that God has granted to the church while living within the guidelines of the principle of authority and being led by the Spirit, many will be delivered, healed, and saved. The devil would have to leave.

When we resist him on these grounds, he must flee. When we resist him steadfast (continually, firmly, and unwaveringly) in the faith, his work is severely damaged (I Peter 5:8-9). And when the power of God is manifested, people will be attracted to it and be converted. "Lord, help us as the church to rise up in Your great authority and power and destroy all the works of the Devil. Anoint us to resist him steadfast in the faith. In Jesus' mighty name."

Signs Are Symbols of the Wonders

We should also understand a difference between signs and wonders. A sign is a symbol of something. It gives you a message that you might not have been able to tell otherwise. In the supernatural world, signs work the same way. If someone has a back problem causing him or her terrible back pain and he or she is prayed for so that the pain leaves, I believe that the back problem has also been healed and made right. The pain leaving the back was sign that the wonder (the back problem being healed) has also been performed. I do not believe that God works like Tylenol, simply as a painkiller. God is more than just in the pain-killing business. He is a healer. He takes care of the problem.

> Four days after the service, a man came up to me and said, "I want you to know what you did to my wife." The worst ran through my mind.

I was in a service in Phoenix where the Holy Ghost impressed me to pray for healing for a certain lady. The lady, named Sister Vasquez, came up to be prayed for concerning her high blood pressure and sugar diabetes. The high blood pressure was causing pain in her chest (for some reason beyond my knowledge). We prayed the prayer of faith and the Lord healed her. Immediately, the pain left. I told her that it was a sign that the wonder had also been performed. We did not receive a sign concerning her sugar diabetes but I told her that I believed that she was healed of it as well. That was all I said.

Four days after the service, a man came up to me and said, "I want you to know what you did to my wife." He explained who his wife was, how I had prayed for her, and what I had told her. The worst ran through my mind. He said that she had been using heavy doses of insulin for nine years and was not able to eat any sugar. After she felt the touch of God she determined to try out her miracle. She immediately quit taking any of the insulin and began to eat a variety of cake, ice cream, candy, and many sodas. The worst really began to run through my mind now.

But she had not had any problems whatsoever. Her blood pressure had gone down to normal according to tests and the level of sugar in her blood was okay. I was relieved and told him to thank God for the miracle but to tell his wife not to run her miracle into the ground. The point is that God did more than simply stop the pain; He took care of the problem.

In another incident, a lady in Washington (named Sister Douglas) had asked for prayer on a Wednesday night because of pain throughout her whole body and primarily in her chest area. She had already had one lung removed and had a history of respiratory problems. The day before our service she had gone to the doctor because of the pain and had some x-rays taken. We prayed and immediately the pain left. I told her it was a sign that the wonder had been performed. The next day the doctor called her to come in because the results of the x-rays showed she had pneumonia. Much to their surprise, when she came in, they found that she had recovered completely. God had already healed her before the doctor even knew what was going on! God is more than simply a painkiller. He is our healer.

> God had already healed her before the doctor even knew what was going on!

Warning Against Unbelief

I believe there is a difference between being faithless or doubting and unbelief. Having no faith is bad enough. Jesus rebuked the disciples repeatedly for having little or no faith. But unbelief is when, like some of the Pharisees and Sadducees, you refuse to believe. In many cases where there was a lack of faith in Scripture, Jesus still performed the miracle, although He rebuked their lack of faith. But when they manifested unbelief – a refusal to be convinced – that was when He refused to work (Matthew 13:53-58).

There are many sincere Christians today who are lacking in faith. God will still work for them in certain instances. There is still hope that they can develop faith. But for those who refuse to believe the reports of miracles or the Word of God, they are guilty of unbelief. This includes those "Christians" who argue that miracles are not for today and/or are only manifestations of the devil's power. They have gone below having zero faith to having negative faith. They are in danger of eternal damnation.[67]

There are some Christians who view various "healing ministries" with skepticism. This could be understandable, knowing the weakness of humanity and the hypocrisy of some. But some dare to go so far as to refuse to believe even when presented with testimonies and the evidence of God's power at work. They may dismiss such things as coincidences (It's amazing that when you stop praying with faith, the coincidences stop happening). You can choose either to have faith and believe or you can choose to refuse to believe in the healing ministry of the church or a man of God despite the signs and wonders manifestly evident. But beware lest you "be found even to fight against God" (Acts 5:39). We do not want to be found in the camp of those classified as "unbelievers." Eternity is too long.

---

[67] See Matthew 12:22-31, Mark 3:22-30, Hebrews 3:7-12, 17-19, 4:1-3, Revelation 21:8.

CHAPTER NINE

ABUSING SPIRITUAL AUTHORITY

The Sin of Limiting God

There is a danger of limiting God by our lack of faith. In Psalm 78, the psalmist begins writing in verse nine about Ephraim. They had turned back in the day of battle. They had not kept the covenant of God, refused to obey Him, and even forgot the works that God had done for them. He begins to describe the great things God had done for them in delivering them from Egypt. He led them through the Red Sea. He led them through the wilderness with a pillar of cloud by day and a pillar of fire by night. He gave them water to drink out of a rock. Then in verses 17-20 it says,

> "They sinned yet more against him by provoking the most High in the wilderness. And they tempted God in their heart by asking meat for their lust. Yea, they spake against God; they said, Can God furnish a table in the wilderness? Behold, he smote the rock, that the waters gushed out, and the streams overflowed; can he give bread also? Can he provide flesh for his people?"

They limited God by not exercising faith in Him. They lived in their doubt. They knew God had done other great works but doubted whether He could do the next thing.

What was God's response? Verses 21-22 says, "Therefore the Lord heard this, and was wroth: so a fire was kindled against Jacob, and anger also came up against Israel; Because they believed not in God, and trusted not in his salvation." God was angry with them because they did not believe in Him. Dare we think that God is any different today when He said, "I am the LORD, I change not"? He still is upset when His people will not believe in Him. God is looking for us to exercise our faith. He's looking for every opportunity to show Himself strong in behalf of those whose heart is perfect (complete) toward Him (II Chronicles 16:9). He wants to demonstrate His power. He desires that we grow in faith.

> They limited God by not exercising their faith.

The psalmist even classified their not believing in God as sin in verse 17. He continues from verse 23 to 31 telling about all God had done. He had fed them with manna and fed them the quail. Yet, "For all this, they sinned still, and believed not for his wondrous works." What was their sin? It was the fact that they refused to believe.

Verse 41 says that "they turned back and tempted God, and limited the Holy One of Israel." They limited God in that they did not exercise faith in Him. And their lack of faith in God was counted as sin. Your faith in God can be counted for righteousness as it did for Abraham (James 2:23, Romans 4:19-22). On the other hand, your lack of faith in God will be counted as sin as it did for the Israelites in the wilderness. "Whatsoever is not of faith is sin" (Romans 14:23). "Lord, help us to exercise faith in you."

The Bible says that God is "able to do exceeding abundantly above all that we ask or think, according to the power that worketh in us" (Ephesians 3:20). There is nothing that God cannot do. With Him, all things are possible. Nothing is impossible with God. But He is only able to do far beyond above all that we ask or think "according to the power that worketh in us." To the degree that we will allow that Holy Ghost power to work in us, to that degree God is able. If that power is not working in us, then we limit God from working, from being able to do all the great things that He can do. Oh, my friend, let faith work.

God Looks for Faith

God does not simply respond to need alone. This is seen in the story of Jesus walking on the water (Mark 6:45-52). The disciples in the boat were struggling in rowing the boat against the wind. The Bible says that He "would have passed by them." But when they cried out, that was when He went to them into the ship and the storm ceased. If God responded only to needs, He would not have passed by them because they needed help. But God is looking for someone to exercise faith.

If God responded only to needs, then He would heal all those in the hospitals because they need help. But God is looking for someone to exercise faith, to believe in Him. He is looking for someone who will not limit Him by his or her lack of faith.

If we do not exercise faith, it is counted as sin. The whole Christian life is based on faith in God. "Whatsoever *is* not of faith is sin" (Romans 14:23). "Take heed, brethren, lest there be in any of you an **evil heart of unbelief**, in departing from the living God" (Hebrews 3:12). A heart of unbelief is described as being evil. Along with the abominable, murderers, whoremongers, sorcerers, idolaters, and all liars that will have their part in the lake of fire (the second death) will also be the "fearful and unbelieving" (Revelation 21:8). "Lord, save us from unbelief."

> Your faith can be counted for righteousness or your lack of faith will be regarded as sin.

Unbelief Is Costly

Unbelief is what kept the Israelites out of the Promised Land for forty years. Concerning them, the writer of Hebrews wrote:

> "For some, when they had heard, did provoke [they provoked God to anger]: ... But with whom was he grieved forty years? Was it not

with them that had sinned, whose carcases fell in
the wilderness? And to whom sware he that they
should not enter into his rest, but to them that
believed not? So we see that they could not enter
in because of unbelief" (Hebrews 3:16a, 17-19).

They had heard the gospel preached (Hebrews 4:2) but it
did not help them. Why? "The word preached did not profit them,
not being mixed with faith in them that heard it." We must
likewise exercise faith when we hear the word of God lest it be of
no profit to us. Hebrews 4:1 says, "Let us therefore fear, lest, a
promise being left us of entering into his rest, any of you should
seem to come short of it." **We must believe.**

God Can and Will

For us not to believe in God is still considered sin. When
you do not exercise faith in God you are questioning the reliability
of His Word. The Word of God explicitly tells us that "with God,
all things are possible" (Mark 10:27). The Bible teaches us that
God is omnipotent; that He always has been, still is, and always
will be the Almighty (Revelation 1:8). There is nothing that He
cannot do. In Genesis 18:14, He asked, "Is any thing too hard for
the LORD?" In Jeremiah 32:27, He claimed, "Behold, I am the
LORD, the God of all flesh: is there any thing too hard for me?" In
verse 17, Jeremiah had prayed, "There is nothing too hard for
thee."

For the Word of God to be profitable to us, it must be mixed with faith. For the gospel of Jesus Christ to help us, it must be mixed with faith.

There is no realm of impossibility with Him. In Numbers 23:19, Balaam told Balak, "God is not a man, that he should lie; neither the son of man, that he should repent: hath he said, and shall he not do it? Or hath he spoken, and shall he not make it good?" The great Apostle Peter declared, "The Lord is not slack concerning his promise, as some men count slackness" (II Peter 3:9a). Hebrews 6:18 states that it's impossible for God to lie. God's Word is clear.

He has made His claims to what He can do. No one should doubt His ability. He has also promised what He will do. "Whatsoever ye shall ask in my name, that will I do, that the Father may be glorified in the Son. If ye shall ask any thing in my name, I will do it" (John 14:13-14). "If ye abide in me, and my words abide in you, ye shall ask what ye will, and it shall be done unto you" (John 15:7). "This is the confidence that we have in him, that, if we ask any thing according to his will, he heareth us: And if we know that he hear us, whatsoever we ask, we know that we have the petitions that we desired of him" (I John 5:14-15). "Ask, and it shall be given you; seek, and ye shall find; knock, and it shall be opened unto you: For every one that asketh receiveth; and he that seeketh findeth; and to him that knocketh it shall be opened" (Matthew 7:7-8).

As long as we will ask in faith, it is possible. Mark 9:23 says that "all things are possible to him that believeth." If only we will have faith, even if it is "faith as a grain of mustard see, ye shall say unto this mountain, Remove hence to yonder place; and it shall remove; and nothing shall be impossible unto you" (Matthew 17:20).

Excuses of Those Lacking Faith

There are some who say that it is not God's will to heal them of a particular sickness or affliction. Is this true? Could they in fact be limiting God by their doubt and lack of faith?

It is amazing to note the types of excuses they will use in an attempt to disguise their unbelief and provide a way to hold on to their faithless heart. They may say, "I have this disease because God is trying to teach me something." Frankly, if I was in their shoes, I would hurry up and learn the lesson before the disease kills me.

> Some maintain, "I have this disease because God is trying to teach me something." Frankly, if I was in their shoes, I would hurry up and learn the lesson before the disease kills me.

Or they may claim, "This sickness is really a blessing in disguise." Is that so? Then why are they spending all that money to buy medicine and see doctors to try and get rid of the blessing? In fact, if it really is a blessing, why don't they just ask God for a double portion of that blessing?

I believe that usually it is just a case of limiting God – something that angers God. They either don't want to exercise faith or are afraid to try. Either way, they question the accuracy of the Word of God.

Thorn in the Flesh

Often, I hear how a particular infirmity is "my thorn in the flesh." Since many have a misconception concerning this, let us look a little closer at II Corinthians 12 where Paul talks about this. First of all, we do not know for sure that Paul's thorn in the flesh was a physical condition. I have heard and read of respected scholars who thought it was among a variety of other things.

Among these other opinions is one that says it refers to the condition of his home, with Paul's wife having left him. Another theory states that it was the Judaizers who constantly plagued his ministry, destroying some of the fruit for which he had worked so hard. I have probably heard or read of a half a dozen different theories. But just for the sake of argument, I will concede that it may have been a physical condition, probably an eye disease. Let us look at the surrounding circumstances.

> If your sickness truly is a wonderful blessing in disguise, why don't you ask God for a double portion of your blessing?

First of all, Paul was one of the greatest apostles. He saw many signs and wonders performed along with tremendous acts of God on his behalf. He saw much revival and growth to the church through his ministry. He was used by God eventually to write about half of the New Testament.

Next, let us look at the surrounding verses. In the previous chapter, Paul described all that he had been through in his service for God. More than most, he had worked hard and sacrificed much. He had received numerous stripes from beatings. He was thrown in prisons. He was beaten with rods three times. Once, he was stoned. Three times he suffered shipwreck. He had traveled many miles on horseback, by ship, and on foot. He often had his life in danger because of sea travel, robbers, his own countrymen, and foreigners. He was in peril in metro areas, in wild wilderness, and because of false brethren. He had endured hunger and thirst. At times, he was cold and naked. All this was in addition to his daily responsibilities to take care of the churches.

Then, in Chapter 12, he talks about some tremendous visions and revelations that he had received from God. This even included what seemed to be "out of body" experiences where he went into the "third heaven." He learned things that were so phenomenal and amazing that he could not speak of it. Considering how awesome and deep his writings in the New Testament are, these revelations must truly have been out of this world. Then the key verse (7) says, "And lest I should be exalted above measure through the abundance of the revelations, there was given to me a thorn in the flesh, the messenger of Satan to buffet me, lest I should be exalted above measure."

Twice in that single verse he says, "lest I should be exalted above measure." My question to those who claim to have a thorn in the flesh is, what great miracles has God done through you that you require a thorn in the flesh just to keep you humble? What great revival have you brought to your country or city or what tremendous signs from God have you seen that you need a thorn in the flesh to help you retain humility? What deep revelations have you been given or what phenomenal visions have you seen that you require a thorn in the flesh? Have you been to the third heaven and heard unmentionable things that you require a thorn in the flesh just to keep you humble? What have you endured in persecutions, hardships, and danger that you require a thorn in the flesh just to keep you from being lifted up with pride?

I believe most of the time people say such a foolish and boastful statement that they are just making an excuse for their lack of faith. They don't have the faith in the Word of God for their healing or deliverance so they conjure up some "spiritual reason" why they are not healed. They try to put the blame on God saying that they are not healed because "it is not His will." If they are not healed it is usually because they have either a lack of faith, have unrepented sins in their lives, or because they have an unforgiving spirit and are holding a grudge or a root of bitterness in their heart against someone.

Let us not limit God. Let us show the world what a great God He really is. Unshackle your faith. Let it be released. Allow God to be God. Let His Word be exalted in your life by receiving it with faith. Don't limit God. Let Him be what He wants to be. Let Him do what He wants to do. Mix faith with the Word of God. Let the awesome power of the Word of God become profitable to you and productive in your life.

Selfish Uses of Authority

Just because we recognize that we have tremendous authority to use the power of God does not mean that we can use it in any way we see fit. We do not have the right to ask for any thing that we desire (in our flesh) just because we want it. You can go overboard with the doctrine of the authority of the believer and say that all you have to do is ask God for a new Cadillac by next Tuesday and it will come. To believe this is to view God as our slave. He is not our slave. He is not our genie out of the bottle. He is our God. We are His people. We are to work as His servants.

> When you ask God for something just to satisfy your own lust, you are tempting God.

Jesus told Satan, "It is written again [quoting Deuteronomy 6:16], Thou shalt not tempt the Lord thy God" (Matthew 4:7). Going back to the children of Ephraim, Psalm 78:18 says, "They tempted God in their heart by asking meat for their lust." They tempted God when they asked something simply to satisfy their lust.

When you ask God for something just to satisfy your own lust, you are tempting God. James 4:3 says, "Ye ask, and receive not, because ye ask amiss, that ye may consume it upon your lusts." If we ask simply to satisfy our fleshly lusts, we have no guarantee that we will receive our request. But if we will ask according to the will of God, we have confidence that He will hear us. And if He hears us, we know He will answer us (I John 5:14-15).

Satan tried to get Jesus to use His great power to sensationalize His standing as the Son of God. He told Jesus to cast Himself down from the pinnacle of the temple. He reasoned that the Word of God promised that He would give angels charge over Him to keep Him from even dashing His foot against a stone. Jesus rebuked the Devil saying that it was also written, "Thou shalt not tempt the Lord thy God" (Luke 4:12).

We also tend to tempt God when we refuse to get our heart right with Him. After the children of Ephraim returned to God in Psalm 78:34, God forgave them and did not destroy them. Still, He was not pleased with them. Verses 36 and 37 say, "Nevertheless they did flatter him

> We are guilty of tempting God when we refuse to get our heart right with Him.

with their mouth, and they lied unto him with their tongues. For their heart was not right with him, neither were they steadfast in his covenant." God is looking for people whose heart is right with Him and who will be faithful to His covenant.

In the account in Hebrews 3, the writer said in verses 7-11,

> "(as the Holy Ghost saith, To day if ye will hear his voice, Harden not your hearts, as in the provocation, in the day of temptation in the wilderness: When your fathers tempted me, proved me, and saw my works forty years. Wherefore I was grieved with that generation, and said, They do always err in their heart; and they have not known my ways. So I sware in my wrath, They shall not enter into my rest.)"

They erred in their heart. Their heart was not right with God. They did not know His ways or the principles by which God operated. So for those that believe that God must do as they say, that all they have to do is "Name it and claim it" or "Blab it and grab it," they have misunderstood how God operates. They have not known His ways. They are erring in their heart.

> God is not our slave. He is not our genie out of the bottle.

They cannot expect to receive when they ask to win the lotto or ask God's blessings on their tavern that they own. God will not bless your whorehouse business because it is not pleasing to Him. Our requests cannot be manipulative just to get what we want. We do not have control over the elements of nature so we can use it at our slightest whim and fancy. But if we are walking before God and doing the work of God, we can even control the weather.

Authority to Control Nature

I remember one time as a teenager that a friend and I were out knocking on some doors for outreach when it began to rain. We ran under a carport and decided that since we were doing the work of God, we could rebuke the rain and continue on until we finished. So we commanded it to stop raining. Within seconds it stopped raining. But the battle was not over yet.

When we started to leave the carport, it started to hail pretty heavily. We ran the approximately one hundred yards back to the carport (it was a rural area) and prayed again. This time we were specific enough to bar any form of precipitation or interference with what we were doing. Again, within seconds it stopped and we continued on our way knocking on doors. When we were through and had made it safely back to his home, we gave the black clouds permissions to continue raining or doing whatever it was supposed to do.

In a moment it was raining again. Was it a coincidence? Perhaps. But maybe not. I believe we had tapped into a realm of spiritual authority. However, we were not praying to stop the rain just because we wanted to play football a little longer. It was to benefit the kingdom of God. We were doing the will of the Father. Therefore, we received what we asked for. This controlling of the weather has happened a number of times with me. Yet, it was never simply for the satisfying of the flesh.

Our hearts must be right with God. Then and only then can we expect to receive what we ask from God. Yes, we can even exercise control over the elements of nature if we are sensitive to the voice of God and are following Him. "If ye abide in me, and my words abide in you, ye shall ask what ye will, and it shall be done unto you." Let His Word live in you. Continue in the presence of God. Exercise the authority of the believer. The promise is ours to claim. The authority is ours to use.

APPENDIX

AUTHORITY OVER DEMONIC PRINCES

We must use the spiritual authority given to the church if we want to see mighty revival in our cities or nations, regardless of our field of service. Since there are certain demonic ruling powers in every geographic area, we must take authority and dominion over them to bind them so that the people within their domains may be delivered on a more wide scale basis. Although this thesis is not intended as a manual for what is often referred to as "spiritual warfare," a quick synopsis will be given.

John Dawson stresses the importance of exercising control over demonic powers ruling over certain geographical areas.

> "Unless you understand biblical warfare you will be frustrated, angry, confused and ineffective in your ministry to the city.... We need to bind the strong man and gain a place of authority over Satan before we will see the full fruit of our labors."[68]

---

[68] John Dawson, 70.

He explains that prayer and fasting is a strong part of what gives a Christian authority and power over the ruling demonic powers. "There is a high price to be paid in personal discipline, prayer and obedience."[69] This does not mean that you fast for power from God; it has already been granted to the church. But it will help you to be more sensitive to the Spirit, if done properly. There are many other things to be said about fasting but I will leave it as it stands.

The Prince of an Area

To find out which power from hell is the prince of the city, one must exercise the gift of discernment. As a confirmation to conclusions, you may see what is the predominant sin in that society. A demonic prince in an area is recognized by the strongholds in the people's mindset. It is what controls and heavily influences the thoughts of people in that area. This is usually the nature, the strongpoint, the specialty, the area of greatest skill of the prince of the city. One can also see approximately when that prince gained control over the city or nation by looking at history. But this should only be used in confirmation to the leading and guidance of the Holy Spirit.

> We can spend time putting out the little fires that various demonic spirits are starting or we can catch the arsonist and get rid of the root of the problems.

Personally, I have found this looking at history to be very relieving. I found out that what the Holy Ghost had told me about the ruling powers of my home state was confirmed by the history books, even as specifically as the date God told me during which that demonic power took control. It was also gratifying to see this principle confirmed by Dawson. "A study of history can give us clues as to God's purpose for a city, and it can also reveal the point at which evil gained entrance."[70]

One note of caution is that we must not try to right every political issue that there is. We are not a political force, though where politics are involved, we should stand for righteousness. I

[69] *Ibid.*, 141.
[70] *Ibid.*, 81.

am not saying Christians should be uninvolved in the political process. On the contrary, Christians must get involved. But the authority of the church lies in the spreading of the gospel of Jesus Christ and the evangelizing of the world, not in some political movement. This has to do with recognizing the boundaries of our authority. Our authority does not yet encompass setting up an earthly kingdom.

> We can spend our time chasing down the issues of the time or we can deal with the commission given to us by the Almighty.

In trying to gain spiritual authority over a city, we can spend our time chasing down the issues of the time or we can deal with the commission given to us by the Almighty. We can spend time putting out the little fires that various demonic spirits are starting or we can catch the arsonist and get rid of the root of the problems. We must recognize that behind the major problems we face are the works of evil spirits. Let us begin to exercise authority and power over them and the problems will begin to right themselves.

The Value of Unity

The unity of the church is also of extreme importance in exercising authority over the princes of various geographical areas. Again, Dawson notes, "Restoring unity between our city's churches is an important part of rebuilding the wall."[71] There are many cities where there are more than one church that believe and preach truth but that do no live in peace and harmony with each other because of envy, politics, pride, or other such reasons. They are not able to see the kind of citywide revival that God is looking to send to them because of the division in the body. Division in the body is like a nervous system that will not work properly. Hearts must be cleansed, bitterness abandoned, and unity restored.

We must not allow our pride to get in our way of asking a brother for forgiveness and righting a wrong. We must also not fall into the trap of not forgiving another because the lack of forgiveness on the part of one Christian gives the devil an advantage over a certain part of the body of Christ (II Corinthians

---

[71] *Ibid.*, 82.

2:10, 11). We should note that the writer of Hebrews explained how a root (singular) of bitterness would cause many (more than one) to be defiled (Hebrews 12:15). Unforgiveness is detrimental to the exercise of spiritual authority.

Search should also be made to see that the beginning of the church was not started in rebellion or in causing other hard feelings. If this is found to be the case, humility should be exercised in officially repairing the breach and being obedient to the Word in asking for forgiveness. Competition in the body of Christ, although in and of itself is not wrong, if it be to the destruction of the church, is not pleasing to God.

Humility about Our Personal "Power"

Dawson also emphasizes that we ought to recognize where we came from. We are a product of all those who have gone before us plus the personal relationship that we have with God. We should remember that others have had a great part, either directly or indirectly, in bringing us to where we are now, whether we realize it or not. It helps to know the history of the type of ministry we are involved in and the history of our movement.

It is not only a matter of getting to the place where we can trust God; there are quite a few who have come to this place in God. We must also mature to the point where God can trust us with the exercise of His great authority and power.

Somebody helped us get to where we are. This knowledge acts to keep us in a spirit of humility. Pride will be a degenerating factor in our spiritual authority if we give it any place. "Our spiritual authority is proportional to our humility and dependence on God."[72] We must be dependent on God, not our own authority.

The authority that God has granted to the church is complete. Colossians 2:10 says that we "are complete in Him." Colossians 2:9 tells us that all the fulness of the Godhead continues to dwell in Jesus. The head of anything refers to the source and seat of authority and power. The fullness of the authority and power of God resided and continues to reside in

---

[72] *Ibid.*, 175.

Jesus. He is the "head of all principality [a form of authority] and power [*exousia* – better understood by the modern use of the word 'authority']" (Colossians 2:10).

Although the authority of the church is complete, we as individuals do not always have that complete authority. The reason is that the Holy Ghost "can only exercise an authority proportionate to the yieldedness of the human vessel."[73] If we are not led by the Spirit of God, we will not know what God is trying to do. Our prayers can only be heard to the extent that we have yielded ourselves to Him (Joshua 3:5, Psalm 66:18, John 15:7). It is the effectual, fervent prayer of a **righteous** man that avails much (James 5:16). It is not only a matter of getting to the place where we can trust God; there are quite a few who have come to this place in God. We must also mature to the point where God can trust us with the exercise of His great authority and power.

Just so we remember it is not our own authority that we are exercising over the powers of hell, we should have a good understanding of the doctrine of the grace and mercy of God, not only for initial salvation but also

> Too often I have seen someone get puffed up with pride because God used him or her one time. The key is to be used of God repeatedly.

for the continuing life of the Christian. Dawson humbly acknowledges, "The fact that He had used me once to gain a victory was a manifestation of His sovereignty and grace, not evidence of any qualifying ability of mine."[74]

Too often I have seen someone get puffed up with pride because God used him or her one time. God used a donkey once. He used a burning bush once. He used a witch in Endor once. The key is to be used of God repeatedly.

Conquering the Foe

Dawson outlines five major steps for victory over evil spirits.[75] They are:

---

[73] *Ibid.*, 187.

[74] *Ibid.*, 107

[75] For more information on tearing down Satan's strongholds, see Part II of my book, *The High Places* (Roanoke, VA: Spirit of Life Press, 1999).

1) Worship. Worship opens us up to the awesome power of God as we realize who He is. When we recognize who He actually is and the power that He holds, it increases our faith.

2) Waiting on the Lord for insight. We are not to rely on our own understanding but to allow the Lord to speak to us, listening with childlike dependency. We can step out by our own zeal and there will be an element of success. However, we can only have true and lasting success and victory if we are led by the Spirit of God. He will give us a battle plan that will not fail.

3) Identifying with the sins of the city. This is shown to us by the examples of Nehemiah (Nehemiah 1:5-9) and Daniel (Daniel 9:1-19). This is a part of the reason why we want to officially repair the broken walls if the church we take over was started in rebellion.

4) Overcoming evil with good. Instead of rewarding evil for evil, we are to overcome the forces of evil with good works (Romans 12:21). Dawson teaches that this means acting in the opposite spirit with whom we are fighting. If it is a spirit of greed and selfishness, we combat it with much giving and generosity. We destroy lust with concentration on purity. We overcome pride with true humility before God. We conquer fear with faith which works by love (Galatians 5:6) which casts out all fear (I John 4:18).

5) Travailing until birth. We must be willing to intercede regardless of what we may come up against. We cannot give up midway through the fight. A child is waiting to be born. Fight to the finish. We must be consumed with a holy passion that will not allow us to settle for anything less than complete victory.

To this I would add a focus on truth. It would be easy to be deceived without having truth as a guide. In our spiritual battles, Paul exhorts us to have our loins girt about with truth (Ephesians 6:14). As long as we have truth that guards our heart, God will see to it that we are not led astray. Our hearts must be thoroughly honest. We must speak the truth in our hearts (Psalm 15:2) for God desires truth in the inward parts (Psalm 51:6).

In addition, we must be involved in the exercise of faith. If we get lazy about exercising our faith, it opens the door for fear, negativity, doubt, and unbelief to move in and take control. It is with the shield of faith that we can quench all the fiery darts of the wicked (Ephesians 6:16).

Dawson states, "The level of a spiritual victory for your city is directly affected by two spiritual conditions: the intensity of your desire and the size of your faith."[76] I agree. Are you willing to settle for a substitute or do you want the real thing? How intense is your desire? How strong is your faith? Do you want a model of revival or the actual process in living color?

> If we get lazy about exercising our faith, it opens the door for fear, negativity, doubt, and unbelief to move in and take control.

Truly, there are times when deliverance or victory is a process, when we must patiently endure until we obtain the promise given to us as Abraham did (Hebrews 6:15). This enduring process can be the forming of Christ in us until God can better trust us with the proper exercise of His authority and power.

Remember, before there can be a resurrection, there must be a cross. "Many dreams die on the road to resurrection power."[77] As it happened with Gideon, the Lord may subtract before He multiplies the victory. Let all who are involved in the work of God begin exercising spiritual authority under the guidelines of the principle of authority so that we may see greater revival and growth to the body of Christ.

Go ahead. Let your faith loose. Exercise your authority as a believer. Demonstrate the power of God.

---

[76] *Ibid.*, 204.
[77] *Ibid.*, 215.

Dear fellow Christian,

I hope this book has, in some way, enlightened and inspired you to do the works of Jesus Christ. If you would like to respond in any way, you may do so at the following address:

Spirit of Life Ministries
4830 Morwanda Dr.
Roanoke, VA 24017

An order form for more materials is found on the next page. Thank you and may the Lord shine wonderfully on your life.

David Sanzo

OTHER MATERIALS BY DAVID SANZO
Please send to:
Spirit of Life
4830 Morwanda Dr.
Roanoke, VA 24017

Order Form

BOOKS: **Qty.**   **Total**

Power to Tread on Serpents   ($8)   _____   _____
    Understanding and Using
    Spiritual Authority

The Key to the Kingdom   ($10)   _____   _____
    Beginning Your Reign
    in the Spirit

The High Places   ($10)   _____   _____
    Prayerfully Rising through
    the Seven Dimensions of Life

SPEAKING TAPES:
($22 per Cassette Album)

Unlocking the Chains that Bind Us   _____   _____
    (Album One – 6 Cassette Tapes)
        1. Trial of Shame
        2. Real Change
        3. Destroying the Works
            of the Devil   (Part I)
        4. Destroying the Works
            of the Devil   (Part II)
        5. Power over Genetics
        6. The Lordship of Jesus Christ

	Qty.	Total

Opening the Doors to New Realms   _____   _____
   (Album Two – 6 Cassette Tapes)
     1. His Excellent Greatness
     2. Get Your Eyes
       on the Supernatural
     3. The Wind of God
     4. Followers of God
     5. A More Excellent Sacrifice
     6. In Spite Of

Releasing the Power   _____   _____
   (Album Three – 6 Cassette Tapes)
     1. Breaking through the
       Barriers
     2. Spiritual Hearing
     3. Spiritual Authority
     4. Power of a Word
     5. The Failure of Prophecy
     6. The Voice of Triumph

MUSIC:

Amaze Me (Angela Sanzo)
    CD ($15)   _____   _____
    Cassette ($10)   _____   _____

SUBTOTAL: _____

Please add 15% for shipping and handling   _____

Total   _____

(Please allow 4-6 weeks for delivery)